PRAISE

How Can I Let Go if I Don'

"Linda Douty's book, filled with stories
know of the release that comes with letting ....ates the places where we
still hang on, and gives us the tools to take our next step toward freedom.
Reading this book is affirming, challenging, and liberating."
—Jane E. Vennard, author of *A Praying Congregation: The Art of Teaching
Spiritual Practice*

"Charmingly and engagingly written, Douty's candid and conversational
approach will appeal to many seeking relief from themselves and their self-
sustained burdens."
—Phyllis Tickle, compiler, *The Divine Hours*

"The author identifies and offers practical suggestions about some of the
dimensions in the landscape of letting go—an essential ingredient in the
growth process. Even though there is general agreement on the need to let go,
people often cannot identify their attachments. Speaking with wisdom based
on experience, Linda charts some of the why, what, and how to uncover attachments and release them—an important book for spiritual seekers."
—Herbert W. Smith, Ph.D., Professor Emeritus of Psychology, Rhodes College,
Memphis, Tennessee

"Linda Douty has written a wise, compassionate, and comprehensive book
rooted in her own life experience, her appreciation of diverse spiritual mentors,
and her deep commitment to God's way. The 'how of letting go' through awareness, availability, action, allowing, and acceptance offers a profound process for
the journey to responsible freedom. The author's honesty evokes and challenges
readers to proceed hopefully in the art of letting go in our own lives."
—Barbara B. Troxell, Senior Scholar in Spiritual Formation, Garrett-Evangelical
Theological Seminary, Evanston, Illinois

"Linda Douty lets us know that the title of her book emerges from her own life
experience and does this in such an inspiring and practical way that enables us
to find much needed help for our own spiritual pilgrimage."
—Paul Blankenship, Professor Emeritus, Church Historian, Memphis
Theological Seminary, Tennessee

"As Linda Douty tells us the story of her journey she shares the achieved
wisdom that has made her an exceptional spiritual director."
—John McQuiston, author of *Always We Begin Again* and *A Prayer Book for
the Twenty-First Century*

an explorefaith.org book

How Can I Let Go If I Don't Know I'm Holding On?

SETTING OUR SOULS FREE

LINDA DOUTY

To Robert, Blessing on your journey of letting go, Linda Douty

MOREHOUSE PUBLISHING

For my sons,
David and Harrison,
my companions and teachers
on the path of letting go

Copyright © 2005 by Linda Douty

Morehouse Publishing, 4775 Linglestown Rd, Harrisburg, PA 17112

Morehouse Publishing is an imprint of Church Publishing Incorporated.

an explorefaith.org book
Spiritual guidance for anyone seeking a path to God

Cover design by Lee Singer

Library of Congress Cataloging-in-Publication Data

Douty, Linda.
How can I let go if I don't know I'm holding on? : setting our souls free / Linda Douty.
p. cm.
ISBN 0-8192-2132-5 (pbk.)
1. Christian life. 2. Submissiveness—Religious aspects—Christianity. 3. Loss (Psychology)—Religious aspects—Christianity. I. Title.
BV4501.3.D69 2005
248.4—dc22
2005004737

Printed in the United States of America
07 08 09 10   6 5 4 3

Contents

explorefaith.org books: An Introduction

The book you hold in your hand says a lot about you. It reflects your yearning to forge a deep and meaningful relationship with God, to open yourself to the countless ways we can experience the holy, to embrace an image of the divine that frees your soul and fortifies your heart. It is a book published with the spiritual pilgrim in mind through a collaboration of Morehouse Publishing and the Web site explorefaith.org.

The pilgrim's path cannot be mapped beforehand. It moves toward the sacred with twists and turns unique to you alone. Explorefaith.org books honor the truth that we all discover the holy through different doorways, at different points in our lives. These books offer tools for your travels—resources to help you follow your soul's purest longings. Although their approach will change, their purpose remains constant. Our hope is that they will help clear the way for you, providing fruitful avenues for experiencing God's unceasing devotion and perfect love.

www.explorefaith.org
Spiritual Guidance for Anyone Seeking a Path to God

A non-profit Web site aimed at *anyone* interested in exploring spiritual issues, explorefaith.org provides an open, non-judgmental, private place for exploring your faith and deepening your connection to the sacred. Material on the site is rich and varied, created to highlight the wisdom of diverse faith traditions, while at the same time expressing the conviction that through Jesus Christ we can experience the heart of God. Tools for meditating with music, art and poetry; essays about the spiritual meaning in popular books and first-run films; a daily devotional meditation; informative and challenging responses to questions we have all pondered; excerpts from publications with a spiritual message—all this and more is available online at explorefaith.org. As stated on the site's "Who We Are" page, explorefaith.org is deeply committed to the ongoing spiritual formation of people of all ages and all backgrounds, living in countries around the world. The simple goal is to help visitors navigate their journey in faith by providing rich and varied material about God, faith and spirituality. That material focuses on a God of grace and compassion, whose chief characteristic is love.

You have the book, now try the Web site. Visit us at www.explorefaith.org. With its emphasis on God's infinite grace and the importance of experiencing the sacred, its openness and respect for different denominations and religions, and its grounding in the love of God expressed through Christianity, explorefaith.org can become a valued part of your faith-formation and ongoing spiritual practice.

Foreword

These words would not be printed on this page, were it not for the life-giving support of kindred spirits—friends and family who gave me a nudge when I needed it, or perhaps even a suitable shove. Thanks to all of you who said, "Yes, you can," when I was thinking, "No, I can't." Your friendship and encouragement are the heartbeat of this book. You know who you are.

It's impossible to overstate the importance of the calming and competent presence of my editor, Nancy Fitzgerald. Her expertise and unwavering faith in this book steadied me in many unstable moments, and I'm immensely grateful. She's a writer's dream.

Special thanks go to my son David and my wordsmith-sister Anita, who took the time to read every word and offer invaluable feedback, not only on the manuscript, but on my memory of personal events. And to Nancy Morris, English teacher extraordinaire, whose red pencil was wielded lovingly toward my misplaced commas and clauses. Most of all, thank you, Harrison and David, for saying in every way possible, "It's okay to do this, Mom."

Preface

Connecting the Dots

For my yoke is easy, and my burden is light. (Matt 11:30)

For as long as I can remember, I have longed to connect the dots between my highest aspirations and my daily life, between the words I recite in church on Sunday and the life I live on Monday. I'm finding that the only way to close that gap is by letting go of the barriers that block it. Letting go is an intimidating subject, a troubling dilemma for every human being—including me. I am not an authority in the field, nor a theologian, nor a psychologist. I am simply a seeker who has stumbled, often blindly, through the steps of letting go as I try to live with more integrity and authenticity.

My story is not unique. Nor are the intimate stories of those who have generously shared their struggles with me. In fact, all we have to offer are some reflections on what we have experienced—some things that have yielded fruit and plenty that have not. I hope our stories will help you, dear reader, to get in touch with your own story. Take what suits your needs and discard the rest.

The foundation for this quest has been the strength and guidance provided by faith in God—not simply in terms of belief, but also of experience. The name we give to the divine Source is not nearly as important as our relationship to it. This relationship with the Sacred has been the reliable constant, the plumb line, the foundation, and the touchstone of my life, even in the midst of the intellectual dilemmas and life traumas that challenged my deepest beliefs. Most of the spiritual language in this book emerges from the Christian tradition that has both formed and *de*formed me. There were things I was taught through the lens of Christianity that have resonated truthfully in my experience. However, some of that teaching doesn't seem to be consistent with the lens of God as seen through the life of Jesus. I have found deep meaning in plumbing the depths of Christian thought, often questioning and struggling as I go, attempting to test its grace-filled mystery and veracity in everyday moments.

Life provides a constant crucible for this work—a virtual letting-go laboratory. The need to let go nudges us toward wholeness and brings us closer to our core identity as unique and beloved children of God. However, the question I keep hearing from others, even those steeped in biblical knowledge, is this: How can I discover what I'm really clinging to? What does letting go *look* like in my behavior, *feel* like in my emotions? How does it affect my spiritual life? What role does it play in bringing me closer to God and others? And, most urgent of all, *how can I do it?*

Letting go is, in many ways, an art. Webster defines "art" as a skill acquired by experience. That certainly applies in this case. For the more we practice this skill—this art—the more familiar we become with the experience of it; the more familiar the experience, the more skilled we become. Remember what it was like to learn to ride a bike? We fell off, we scraped our knees, we put on Band-aids, and climbed back on. Then gradually, gradually, gradually, it became an automatic part of who we were—natural bike-riders! We can develop the same kind of spiritual "muscle memory" by practicing the art of letting go.

In these pages, I'll explore the tiny letting go's, the monumental letting go's, and the ongoing letting go's—the barriers that not only weigh us down, but also retard our freedom to love unconditionally. Once we identify those barriers, I'll suggest some techniques and tools for dismantling them.

A client who came to me for spiritual direction once remarked in frustration, "My life feels so chaotic, so burdened all the time. I just want my spirit to be *lighter!*"

Is that sense of a springy step, an uncluttered mind, and a soaring spirit really within the bounds of reality? All the great wisdom traditions promise that it is, and we yearn to experience the truth of it. However, as human beings, our spirits buckle under the burden of unrealistic expectations, unhealthy beliefs, unresolved conflicts, harmful patterns—baggage that weighs us down because we just don't know how to let it go.

Many of these "bags" were packed for us by society's expectations. Our culture demands success, our churches demand perfection, our egos demand approval, and we find ourselves lost in a chorus of competing voices.

This book is about lightening that load by examining and eliminating some of the baggage. We can become more aware of what we're holding on to, how it is weighing us down, and most important, how to release it. However, to feel that buoyancy, we must enter the land of letting go. The path there is full of unexpected detours, emotional landmines, and spiritual challenges. But the payoff is a spirit open to love and joy.

The reality is that we never seem to run out of things to let go.

Sometimes we need to let go of a person in order to move on.

Sometimes we cling to a role that no longer has validity in our lives.

Sometimes a point of view blocks our growth.

Sometimes the volume of our own mental and physical clutter threatens to engulf us.

Sometimes an idea about God must be released so that a fuller faith connection can take place.

Sometimes an unrealistic expectation sabotages our joy.

Sometimes hurts and resentments keep us from experiencing the forgiveness of God.

Sometimes the difference between inappropriate worry and responsible concern eludes us.

Sometimes our limited dreams keep us from joining God's grander dream for us.

Sometimes we have to let go of who we *think* we are to discover who we *really* are.

And often we have to let go of our fear of failure and disapproval to answer the insistent call of our souls. That was certainly one of the letting-go challenges confronting me as I began writing this book!

After considering the *why* of letting go, we'll look at *what* we seem to be holding on to. In the final section, I will suggest some specific tools that may be useful in the quest for *how* to let go.

We can't accomplish much by merely mastering the *information* about letting go. We experience the realities through personal struggle, painstaking trial and error, and ragged spiritual formation that miraculously turns to freedom. So don't be afraid to do the inner digging and try the techniques.

It is my hope and my prayer that this book will encourage you to take that journey with me as we practice the art of letting go.

Linda Douty
March 2005

Part I
Letting Go—Why?

Why Am **1** I Stuck?

> But this one thing I do: forgetting what lies behind and straining forward
> to what lies ahead. . . . (Phil 3:13b)

I was determined to get it right this time. As I carried the tiny artificial
Christmas tree into the motel room, I realized my work was cut out for me.
The space looked drab, lifeless, utilitarian. Maybe David's and Harrison's
favorite ornaments, packed away in the boxes I lugged inside, would provide a
familiar touch, a heart connection to the poignant past. I had hauled them all
the way from Texas to Tennessee in a fervent effort to bring some nostalgic
merriment to our Christmas dinner and gift exchange. Come to think of it, it
wasn't even Christmas Day yet—that was a full five days ahead. But this was
the only time slot that could be wedged into the competing schedules of a
divorced family.

It was a far cry from the Currier and Ives celebrations enshrined in my
memory. During those early years, our Tennessee home had been the center of
yuletide gatherings—neighborhood caroling parties, large family reunions,
holiday songfests around the player piano, and always the Christmas Eve family communion service at the church. I was determined to re-create the atmosphere, if not the reality, of those happy holiday occasions, even within the
boundaries of shared custody agreements. Eight years before, I had reluctantly
given up the marriage. But I refused to give up the memories.

David and Harrison, then twenty-two and seventeen, had become accustomed to the Christmas chaos during the four years since I had moved to
Dallas. It had become a frustrating problem in logistics for all of us, but especially for the boys, pulled hither and yon by the needy love of friends and relatives from two families. Though I tried to be especially sensitive to their
discomfort, the truth was that I was also one of the needy ones—maybe the

most needy. This year it was their father's turn to be with the boys on December 25th, but I told myself that it didn't really matter. I would simply summon extra effort and creativity and *invent* a festive environment. I could produce it like a play, choreographing every scene. So I purchased the best chicken dinners Colonel Sanders had to offer, placed them on holly-printed paper plates, and lit the candles. Our time together would be a bona fide Merry Christmas, no matter the makeshift location.

Well, this Christmas concoction in the motel suite was anything but merry. Despite everyone's best efforts, the gathering felt contrived, stilted, phony. We hid behind plastic smiles that said, "We're going to *pretend this is fun!!*" It was as if we were burying—one more time—that recurrent sadness and disappointment and yearning for yuletides past. But deep down the evening felt, at least to me, like just one more thing to get through, another item to check off the holiday list.

Year after year, I had been inventing new activities and trying desperately to follow the advice in the blended family books: "Create new holiday habits!" But my bag of magic tricks was just about empty. I was emotionally exhausted from the effort of producing the perfect substitute Christmas for my children. My stubborn holding-on to unrealistic expectations had me *stuck*. Something had to change. I had to let go of my illusion that by sheer force of will and creativity, I could make everything okay for my sons, not to mention myself. Little did I realize that my desperation was leading me into unfamiliar territory—the land of letting go. I didn't know what I was in for.

Of course, I thought I already knew what letting go was all about. Hadn't I moved from my Tennessee home and confronted the challenges of urban Texas? Hadn't I shed my persona as small town southern belle and leapt into the big-city milieu of Dallas? I may have been conscious of the *external* behaviors of letting go, but the unconscious layers underneath—the *internal* work—was foreign territory to me.

And I was truly stuck, mired in the mud of negativity, looking for a lifeline. So I turned where I had always turned when I was at the end of my rope of independence, when my storehouse of human resourcefulness was bankrupt. I turned to the faith in God that was a part of my very bones and being.

It had been that way for as long as I could remember—all the way back to tortured teen years when I would sneak into the empty church sanctuary in Savannah, Tennessee, and sink to my knees in anguish over a current crisis. I seemed always to be trying to connect the dots between the words in the sermons and the tumult in my life. I wanted the Christian story to make a difference in the way I lived—or else what was the point? The words of Jesus had to have relevance to the day's events; otherwise they seemed like pretty platitudes that were nice to believe but didn't change anything.

How was it possible to be kind to those who excluded me? If I prayed for what I wanted, would God really hear me? Prayer that began as a matter of asking for friends or romance or a college scholarship began evolving into a conversation with a steadfast Friend to whom I poured out my adolescent angst. A part of me knew that there was more to prayer than a laundry list of requests directed to a celestial bell hop, but the mystery of it all confounded me. Even through the doubts about dogma, something hopeful kept persisting. There was an underlying sense of the reality of God in my life that hung on like a dog with a bone—a Love that would not let me go.

As the years passed, life continued to challenge my religious assumptions. And the naïve notion that "If you do good, good will come to you" was sorely tested in the crucible of my divorce. I had wanted nothing quite so much as success as a wife and mother, and my husband's unhappiness in our marriage had devastated my self-esteem. I had tried my best and been found wanting. Or at least that's how it felt to me at the time.

Some parts of the Christian message were like balm to my soul during those terrible months, and some most definitely were not. Friends and family, whose loving care literally glued me back together, were the embodiment of God's divine comfort. They prayed for me, ranted with me, cooked and cleaned my house, helped with the care of my boys—a stunned nine-year-old and an angry fourteen-year-old.

But one question—posed by a well-meaning friend—rearranged the pieces of what I thought I believed. With a voice full of sincere concern, she asked me, "Wonder what God is trying to teach you through this?" I wasn't prepared for the rage that erupted inside me. I was forced to confront my own questions about God's role in the tragedies of our lives. I refused to believe that the God who had been my comforter and friend all those years would engineer painful life events to teach me a lesson. That was not a God I wanted to worship.

It would take years to make my peace with the mysterious relationship between divine providence and free will. I literally had to "live into the answer" and to experience first hand that, indeed, *All things work together for good for those who love God. . . ."* (Rom 8:28). Not all things *are* good, but rather all things can work *toward* good. As I began to redefine my faith—again— another truth emerged. I realized that there would be no end to this "redefining," that we are all works in progress in the hands of a loving and patient God, a God who works *through* the ups and downs of life, not apart from them.

So, here I was again, five days before Christmas, standing on the threshold of yet another life lesson as my boys and I opened the pretty packages with "oohs" and "aahs" and "thank-you's." My well-maintained façade of perfect survivor was beginning to crumble. As soon as this evening was over, I told myself, I would have to figure it out and *fix it.*

Later, I tried to attack the problem in my usual methodical way, by setting reachable goals and developing a plan of action. But it seemed that God had deeper work in mind—the stripping away of more layers of my own reliable defense mechanisms. The challenge wasn't just about control of Christmas. Nor was it merely about a mother's desire to protect her children from pain.

Just what was I holding on to and why? Did I see myself as a victim? Had that become my identity? What payoff was I getting? If I let go of this fierce protectiveness of the boys, did that mean that I was not the mother who could make it okay, soothe every anxiety, bandage every wound? And—the real clinker—was I ready to face my own unconscious contributions to the breakup of my marriage?

As I was climbing off my high horse of perfectionism, God was loosening the soil of other buried illusions and attitudes. Each question led to a deeper layer, ultimately leading away from the surface events to the very center of myself, forcing me to deal with issues of acceptance, surrender, and authentic trust. I didn't realize that honestly facing those questions would take the rest of my life.

So that night in the Old English Inn off Interstate 40, we gobbled up the fried chicken and politely thanked each other for the gifts. We hugged and called out our "Merry Christmases," but I could already feel the beginning of an inner shift in my soul. Something new was emerging. A freer self was lurking behind all the shoulds and oughts and musts. I began to loosen my grip on the past so that new life could be born—whether in a manger or in a motel.

For Reflection

1. Is there a situation in your life where you feel stuck?

2. What are the signs and symptoms of this kind of inertia?

3. What kind of courage is required to pursue self-reflection?

4. Anais Nin once penned these words: "And the day came when the risk to remain tight in a bud was more painful than the risk it took to blossom. . . ." What do you think she meant?

5. When does the risk to remain stuck become more painful than the risk of letting go?

Why Do I Need to Let Go?

Very truly, I tell you, unless a grain of wheat falls into the earth and dies, it remains just a single grain; but if it dies, it bears much fruit. (John 12:24)

I was alarmed at the tone of Aunt Martha's voice on the phone. My cheerful, self-sufficient, eighty-something aunt was the matriarch of the family, a model of independence since being widowed twenty years before. Her usual upbeat demeanor was gone. It was as if her very life had been drained from her.

As I pressed her with more probing questions, she admitted that she had just attended her fourth funeral that week, a memorial service for a Sunday School class member several years her junior. "Guess I'd better find myself some younger friends," she remarked sadly, making a futile attempt at humor.

As I hung up the phone, I realized that her losses were piling up daily. She had been caretaker for her husband until his death, and she nursed my mother, then her mother, then the rest of her siblings. Now her once-full roster of friends had shrunk to just a few, and it seemed their numbers were diminishing daily.

She wasn't simply losing the people in her life; she was losing a *way of life.* She could no longer drive. She could no longer see well enough to read. She had been forced to give up much of her independence. The loss of her younger self had occasioned a host of issues of letting go, from her eyesight to her waistline to her friendships. How had she learned to cope with the acceleration of losses common to old age? While some folks like Martha seemed somehow to assimilate loss, I knew others who railed against it, becoming continual complainers with shriveling souls.

It brought to my mind another recent conversation—one I overheard between my son and daughter-in-law, both medical internists. They were discussing their aging patients, and one said to the other: "It seems as people age, they divide into two camps—those who decide to keep growing and adapting to change and those who stagnate." Like any good mother-in-law, I butted right into their conversation and asked, "What does that look like? What did you notice about these people? How can you tell the difference?"

And they didn't mince any words. "The first group," they explained, "is characterized by openness to change, curiosity, willingness to ask the tough questions. They allow old patterns to be challenged and their future expands into deeper wisdom and growth. In the second group, the opposite occurs. The future contracts into a rigid and passive existence where old patterns harden, where prejudices and judgments and opinions are set in concrete. They don't know how to let go."

David added, "Oh, you know, Mom. People who say things like 'My mind is made up; don't confuse me with the facts' or 'In *my* day' as if they have turf to protect or a stubborn need to be right—people who are *set in their ways.*"

Even modern science is attempting to speak to this common dilemma by studying those who grow old in a positive and meaningful way. The traditional medical lens has focused on "fixing it when it's broken." But now, researchers are beginning to look at the aging process through a different lens. What keeps us well? What makes us happy? What keeps us from becoming both bored and boring? What helps us adjust not only to aging but also to life? We're becoming familiar with terms like preventive medicine, holistic health, and the interaction between mind, body, and spirit. With each investigation and discovery, we're reaching a better understanding of the psalmist's words: ". . . I am fearfully and wonderfully made" (Ps 139:14).

Several years ago, the TV news magazine *20/20* featured a segment on the study of one hundred active centenarians from cultures around the globe. To inspire the rest of us to grow older with zest, the study pinpointed common traits shared by these healthy, productive elders.

It turns out that there was no magic potion. But there were four attributes that all these centenarians shared:

1. a fundamental optimism about people and life in general

2. engagement in some passion (anything from gardening to church work to weaving to teaching)

3. regular physical activity

4. *the ability to adapt to loss, to let go*

Learning to let go may take a lifetime, but contemporary science says it's worth it. As the habits of this select group of high-functioning adults show, one of the serendipities seems to be the ability to live better and longer. The elderly folks in the study had developed ways to release the old in preparation for receiving the new, entering into a basic rhythm of change that is built into creation.

If God created the world in this fashion, doesn't it make sense to get in sync with that intrinsic pattern? People who do tend to live more robust, productive lives that spill over into the lives of others, creating a kind of happy contagion. If loss and gain are built into the very fabric of creation, then perhaps getting into harmony with that reality is an automatic life-enhancer, a win-win situation. This same dynamic is found in the concept of the "helper's high," where both those who give help and those who receive it are beneficiaries of grace. Dealing creatively with loss somehow puts us in harmony with the grand design of creation.

Look around you. The pattern of loss and gain is everywhere! Winter is followed by spring; night is followed by day; death is followed by resurrection. God created everything from galaxies to trees to human beings with inherent cycles of loss and gain. But unlike trees, we humans have the wonderful and terrible gift of free will. We can choose to cooperate with this natural divine process or we can fight against it. We can spend our whole lives refusing to loosen our grasp. No matter how fervently we pray, God will not arbitrarily take away that which we refuse to release.

We usually think of loss and gain in terms of the tangible: *persons* when they die or leave, *places* when we must relocate, or *things* when we attempt to simplify our lives. But the layers of letting go are much more pervasive than that. We're engulfed in a myriad of *in*tangibles that need releasing. What about our attachment to being right, our illusion that the world should be fair, our unspoken requirement that everyone agree with us? Unless we learn the art of these necessary goodbyes and hellos, we risk remaining stuck in patterns that retard our growth and make us miserable.

Developmental Letting Go

Our ability to perceive this pattern and respond to it shapes us from the cradle to the grave. In *Necessary Losses*, Judith Viorst provides a fascinating overview of our developmental changes as human beings.[1] As babies, she writes, we let go of our parents' hands and move into physical independence on unsteady legs. As adolescents we move from the security of home to experience autonomy in the outside world. In middle age we say farewell to our younger selves and move into a new stage of identity. Ultimately, we encounter the final letting go in the experience of death.

Psychological Letting Go

Our psychological selves also expand through the pattern of loss and gain. We discover that our peace of mind is linked with letting go of perfectionism, certainty, fairness, approval, and a host of other perceived psychic needs that can create anxiety. In the pages ahead, we'll take a close look at the ways we cling to these unhealthy habits of thought and behavior.

Spiritual Letting Go

Our spiritual lives are not exempt from the process of loss and gain. Growth in the spirit requires us to move into God's cycles of revelation and transformation, of dying and rising. Our limiting concepts of God must be constantly open to revision as we experience God in ever-expanding ways.

- We let go of "God as harsh critic" so we can fully embrace "God as unconditional love."

- We let go of categories like "either-or" so we can perceive the paradoxes of "both-and."

- We let go of narrow notions of verbal prayer to make room for the mystery of silence.

- We let go of our grasping control of our own agendas to enter the abundance of God's dream for us.

As you read these pages, I hope I have convinced you of the need to consider your own reaction to the pattern of loss and gain that is all around us. The need is as current as your last breath.

- We have to let go of one breath before we can breathe in another one. Our physical health depends on it.

- We have to let go of a negative thought before a positive thought can take its place. Our mental health depends on it.

- We have to let go of a spiritual barrier before God can help us grow in love. Our spiritual health depends on it.

If letting go is such a basic component of our existence as human beings, then why do we have so much trouble doing it? This is what we'll be exploring in the chapters ahead.

For Reflection

1. To which camp do you belong—those committed to continuing growth or those with a tendency to stagnate?

2. What are some recognizable signs of growth and stagnation?

3. Can you think of examples in your life of physical letting go? Psychological letting go? Spiritual letting go?

Why Am I Afraid to Let Go?

> Take delight in the Lord, and God will give you the desires of your heart.
> (Ps 37:4)

What creatures of habit we are—so much so that we hold on to the familiar even when it serves us poorly, even when it keeps us stuck. After all, if we let go of what we know, what would replace it? It's a bit like the flight of the trapeze artist. He lets go of his flying partner and faces a terrifying transition before the next pair of hands appears and he can actually see what's coming. He learns to trust what he cannot yet touch.

There is an old fable called "Once Upon a Puddle," which powerfully (and humorously) illustrates the nature of our fear.

This is a story about some fish who lived in a very small puddle of water. Listen to their conversation.

"Give me that waterbug!"

"No, I saw him first!"

"Get your fins off my supper! He's mine, I tell you!"

And so, every day, the little fish spent their time competing for waterbugs. Their stagnant puddle was cradled between the roots of an ancient oak tree, just beside a flowing river.

But one morning, there was a sudden *splash*!

An amazing, brightly colored fish had jumped into the riverside puddle . . . a fish with golden scales. And—what was *most* unusual in this particular puddle—he was smiling!

One of the puddlefish asked, "Where do *you* come from?"

The Sparkling Fish smiled brightly, "I come from the *sea*!"

"The sea? What's the sea?"

The Sparkling Fish was surprised and said, "No one has ever told you about the sea? Why, the sea. . . the sea is what fish are *made* for! It isn't like this little puddle; it's endless! A fish needn't swim in circles all day . . . he can dance with the tides! And it's sparkling clear! Yes, the sea is what fish are made for!"

Then a pale gray puddlefish spoke up: "But, how do we get to the sea?"

The Sparkling Fish answered: "Oh, it's a simple matter. You just jump from this little puddle into that river and trust that the current will take you to the sea."

Astonishment clouded the puddle water. At long last, a brave little fish swam forward with a hard, experienced look in his eye. He was a Realist Fish.

He said: "It's pleasant to talk about this 'sea business.' But, if you ask me, we have to face reality. And what is reality? Obviously, it's day-to-day life—swimming in circles and hunting for waterbugs. Life is hard. It takes a Realist Fish to face facts."

The Sparkling Fish smiled, "But you don't understand . . . I've *been* there. I've *seen* the sea. And it's far more wonderful than you can . . ." But before he could finish, the Realist Fish swam away.

Next a fish came up with a nervous twitch in his tail. He was a Scared Fish. He stammered, "You mean, we're supposed to j-j-jump into that big, swift river over there? Look, I'm just an ordinary little fish. That river is deep and strong and wide, and besides, I'm not sure where it goes! Why, I might be swept away by the current! If I jumped out of my puddle, I might not have control over my life! No . . . too risky for me . . ."

The Sparkling Fish whispered, "Just *trust me* . . . Trust that the river will take you someplace *good* . . ." But, the Scared Fish hurried away.

Finally, there swam out a very dignified figure in a black robe—a Theologian Fish. Calmly, he adjusted his spectacles, saying: "My brother and sister fish, our distinguished visitor has expressed views which merit our consideration. However, these puddlefish have expressed other views. By all means, let us be reasonable. We can work this out. . . . Why not form a discussion group? We could meet every Tuesday at 7 PM, and I'm sure some of the lady puddlefish would be happy to bring refreshments."

The eyes of the Sparkling Fish grew sad. "No, this will never do. Talking is important, but in the end—it is a simple matter. You *jump*. You jump out of this puddle and trust that the river will take you to the sea. Who will come and follow me?"

At first, no one moved. Then a few puddlefish swam to his side. Together they jumped into the river and the current swept them away to the sea.

The remaining puddlefish began to swim in circles and hunt for waterbugs just like they always had.

Most of us are not so different from the frightened puddlefish. We, too, are afraid to trust the unknown and to release our old habits. We, too, like to be in control and know what's coming. We're even reluctant to believe the promise of Jesus about the "abundant life." We would prefer a photo of it before we sign on!

The puddlefish who stayed with the status quo lacked an essential element necessary to growth—the willingness to take a risk. The story asks us to trust that God is a dynamic reality in our lives, not merely a distant deity worthy of our admiration. Are we telling the truth when we say we "trust God," or are we paying lip service to a belief that is actually disconnected from the way we live?

As we summon the courage to ask ourselves that question, we are sticking our toe in the water. And that's okay. We may not be ready yet to do a swan dive into that river of radical trust. Putting pressure on ourselves with words like "should, ought to, supposed to" only increases our inner resistance and thwarts the process. Asking a probing or unsettling question is itself a leap of faith. The poet Rainer Maria Rilke spoke of the value of such questions in *Letters to a Young Poet*: "Try to love the questions themselves, like locked rooms and like books written in a foreign language. At present you need to live the question. Perhaps you will gradually, without even noticing it, find yourself experiencing the answer, some distant day."[1]

Most of us begin exploring this fear of letting go very slowly and at an early age. As a teen participant in many summer camps that ended in elaborate dedication ceremonies, I remember my fearful reaction to the invitation, "Will you give your life to Christ?" Each of us would light our candle and place it on a paper plate and launch it on the lake. Like a flickering fleet, the plates floated across the water, symbolizing our surrender to Jesus. However, there was an unspoken fear deep inside me each time I let my candle go that if I surrendered in a concrete way, my life as I knew it would be *over*. I would be sent to deepest Africa as a missionary and never be heard from again. No matter the details, it would involve sacrifices that I didn't really want to make. Trust in God came to be tainted by a fear of loss, rather than a belief in gain. Somehow many of us failed to receive the message that God's will for us could actually bring us incredible joy. It could include the very passions and talents and desires that are a part of our humanity.

But before I could even begin to embrace that hopeful notion, I had to let go of my fear. It took many years before I became aware that I was a Scared Fish.

Fear usually sneaks into our lives disguised as something else—a wolf in sheep's clothing. Like the Realist Fish, I have a life pattern of making decisions from the vantage point of my head only, while patting myself on the back for being practical and prudent. Our gut instincts—those visceral tugs at our heartstrings—are rendered powerless by our intellect. I was taught not to trust intuitive understanding that bubbled up from my own soul—*that* was branded as wishful thinking, useless daydreaming, and worst of all, *uncertainty*. Unfortunately, in Christian culture, our inner voice is often regarded as untrustworthy, rather than honored as a part of the "kingdom within" where God whispers to us.

How many life-giving opportunities do we toss aside in pursuit of the pragmatic? My friend Jeffrey, a wizard of words, remains stuck in a robotic profession, while his story notes for a sensational novel grow tattered with age. After all, he's a realist and needs to fulfill his "duties." Fear often lurks behind this familiar curtain of responsibility.

Celeste tried to maintain a dutiful posture in a different way. She and her husband worked for the same company, and even though she was offered promotion after promotion, she secretly declined each one to placate the fragile ego of her husband.

I met a woman at a workshop recently who poured out her impassioned dream of launching her own small business. Sara had researched and planned for years, waiting till just the right time—when everyone else's needs were met. That day mysteriously outdistanced her, as she became accustomed to pushing her plans to the back burner where resentment was disguised as duty. Like the Theologian Fish in our story, she kept "referring it to committee" while the minutes of her life ticked by. Intellect has a useful function in the discernment process, to be sure, but not to the exclusion of the creative call of the soul.

This fearful resistance can wear many disguises. And deceptions. You might think that, since I'm writing a book on this subject, I would have conquered most of my resistance habits. I wish that were true. One day—a day that I had blocked out for "writing only"—I found myself pulling weeds out of the brick sidewalk outside my back door—a job that I utterly despise. And I had to face the fact that, though I clearly *wanted* to write the book, procrastination had become a daily habit. Why was I so resistant?

A basic part of my wiring—a highly structured side—had automatically clicked into place when the term "big project" registered on my brain. I made elaborate schedules—so many pages a day, so many chapters a month—and all plans ended up on the scrapheap. There was constant internal conflict between a commitment to "freedom and flow" and a compulsion to "get the job done." The result was a see-saw of intentions and postponements. I placed countless trivial tasks ahead of putting pen in hand. Friends had offered empty vacation homes for privacy and seclusion, but there was always an excuse not to block the time. I had prudently eliminated many of my extracurricular activities to free up adequate writing time, but I wasn't taking advantage of it. It felt as if there were imaginary chains around me, holding me back, preventing me from jumping into the "flow." I knew what I should do, what I *wanted* to do—so why couldn't I just do it?

This writing dilemma turned into one of the most perplexing letting-go lessons I've dealt with in a long time. At first, I attributed it to laziness, lack of discipline, diversions of other activities, family responsibilities—even age. I could *feel* my resistance, I could see its effects, I could *talk* incessantly about it. But doing the work to *uncover* its origins seemed daunting. Gritting your teeth and pushing through the resistance doesn't usually work if you don't know what stumbling block you're stumbling on. And I sensed that it was more than simply the return of my old nemesis—rigid structure.

When I dug down to the bottom of my resistance, I found *fear*. It was time to explore it, to name it. And I had to get some inkling of the psychological payoff I was getting. Was I trying to garner sympathy and support from others by moaning about the difficult work? Was I trying in some perverse way to make myself seem more important? Was I simply using any available excuse to keep from working? It took some time to discover that, lurking underneath all the resistance, were fears of failure and disapproval. If I exposed some of the truth of my life, what would people say? Would I have to move to Australia and change my name? If I wrote honestly about my deep-seated discomfort with some church doctrines, would my theological friends think me heretical? If those whose intellect I admired felt the book was trite, would I be able to bear their criticism of my work?

Amazingly, the *naming* of the resistance opens the door to the dismantling of it. Awareness of its nature helps to identify it when it rears its stubborn head. My friend Wanda taught me the power of bringing such inner fears to con-sciousness. Her signs of resistance were physical—constricted muscles in her neck, debilitating lower back spasms, teeth clenched with tension. Chaos was reigning in her home, and she was unable to do anything about it—except resist in a way that was literally holding her health hostage. Her husband, though desperately ill, seemed to be waging a battle of defiance against doctor's orders. He seemed determined to live life on his own terms, grabbing each day by the throat and squeezing out every bit of gusto possible. Her dogged attempts to cajole, coax, and even *beg* him to take better care of himself had been soundly rebuffed.

Despite the fact that a tragic accident had left him paralyzed years ago, he had continued to maintain a creative presence of authority at the office, mak-ing critical decisions and barking orders from his motorized, high-tech wheel-chair. Now his decline appeared to be accelerating, and Wanda was frightened and frustrated.

Fortunately, during these difficult years, she had learned that the body speaks to us in myriad ways, giving warning signs of stress. Well, this time her body was *shouting* at her! She knew she had to let go of responsibility for his decisions, but *how*? The implications of his behavior were dire and clearly beyond her control.

Not that she could blame him. He had always been a person who lived life flat-out, a powerful and dominating presence in the business world. After the accident, he had poured himself even more deeply into this work, redoubling his efforts to expand and create new business opportunities, overcoming near-impossible odds. Wanda took a deep breath and recalled her time-tested tools for letting go.

First, she explained, she called it what it was. She talked through the reality of the situation and then *named her own resistance*. She felt the resistance and owned it. Then somehow, the naming that started in her head began to send its healing messages to her body. She enlisted the aid of her breath in the releas-ing process, and the muscles in her aching neck slowly began to loosen. She was participating in the mysterious and miraculous interaction of body, mind, and spirit in which we are created. But, she hastened to add, it was not a cut-and-dried process. It remained an ongoing struggle, a repetitive exercise in letting go. Like the puddlefish, she had to overcome her own fearful resistance as she swam in the puddle of her own experience.

In what ways do we mirror the actions of those who remained stuck, "swimming in circles hunting for waterbugs"? Our human version of this behavior is found in our comfort with doing things like we've always done them, fulfilling what's expected of us, and staying within the bounds of the familiar. And sadly, many of us die with our music still in us, still circling in waters that seem safe and predictable.

Trusting God may sound like a passive activity, as if we were reclining in our spiritual chairs and waiting for God to make it happen, spreading the future clearly before us so we can see what we're getting into. That's rarely the way it evolves. Once we accept the invitation to let go, we must take the first small step, then another and another. In other words, we *participate* in the process. Like the puddlefish, we need the good sense to swim *with* the current, not against it, as we are swept out to the sea.

So, in this risky land of letting go, we enter the process while the outcome is still unclear, with a willingness to forgive ourselves for the inevitable faltering. No matter what has brought you to the brink—a tragedy, a mysterious tension, or simply a feeling of "Is-this-all?"—you are being invited to leap in. And that first "jump" is one of saying *yes* to the process, trusting that God will be with you, even through the choppy waters.

For Reflection

1. Can you identify one thing that keeps you in the status quo, unwilling to risk?

2. Which of the puddlefish types do you identify with most strongly? Why?

3. What would you lose by taking a risk?

4. At this point, what do you think is your greatest resistance to letting go?

Letting Go
What It Is and What It Isn't

Let the same mind be in you that was in Christ Jesus, who, though he was in the form of God, did not regard equality with God as something to be exploited. (Phil 2:5–6)

Process, Not Action

I felt as if I had a spiritual pebble in my shoe—a little rock called restlessness that wouldn't go away. I tightened my prayer disciplines, made sure I didn't neglect my devotional times, signed up for another Bible study, increased my efforts in community projects for the poor. All to no avail. I still had an unnamed spiritual itch.

I had always been a self-starter, thriving on good organization and workable agendas. I knew how to get things done—or so I thought. And I knew that I had to find a solution for my restless spirit. It was making me distracted during prayer time, twitchy during worship services, and feeling generally disconnected from God. I started feeling guilty when I looked at the magnet on my refrigerator that read, "If you don't feel close to God, then guess who moved?"

Yes, there must be something drastically lacking in my spiritual life. It had collapsed in the ditch. Maybe I wasn't as committed as I thought. Had I been pursuing church and charity work for the wrong reasons? In any case, the resident question pounding in my head was: What is *wrong* with me?

Finally, I spilled it all out to my pastor—a good friend and dedicated champion of the poor and marginalized. He sat patiently through my rambling, convoluted speech, then said reassuringly, "You'll be fine, Linda—you just need to get back to the church work that you've loved all these years, things that you're really good at. By the way, the stewardship campaign is coming up soon, and I could use your help. You and I could meet with the consultant next week and . . ."

I didn't hear the rest of his pitch because I could feel the tears stinging behind my eyelids, an involuntary response to the feeling that I hadn't really been heard. His response, though well-intended, confirmed my assumption that there really WAS something wrong with me after all. What started as a minor irritation—that spiritual pebble in my shoe—began to feel more like a gnawing in the pit of my stomach, as if I had accidentally skipped lunch. Though I didn't know its name at the time, I was experiencing an intense hunger for God.

But hadn't I been in the church all my life? Hadn't I sung the hymns, recited the creeds, chaired the committees, tried to be a worthy disciple? What was missing? To fill in the missing piece, of course, I signed up for more courses, bought some more books by spiritual experts. They would surely provide a cure for my malaise. But nothing seemed to satisfy the longing. Psalm 42 resonated in my mind, "As a deer longs for flowing streams, so longs my soul for you, O God."

As the hunger became more insistent, louder, more disruptive of my peace and contentment, I tried to explore the feelings, figure it out. Somehow in my frantic work in trying to get it right for God, I felt as if I'd been working for Someone—striving to complete the tasks, work the territory, prove myself worthy of employment. I had read the rules, agreed to company policy, and carried out my assignments, but didn't really *know* the object of my allegiance. I had not actually experienced a close relationship with my "employer." Relationship with God was a phrase that I uttered, not a connection that I actually felt. I was beginning to sense the gap, but I couldn't find a way to bridge it.

At that point, a monumental grace entered my life in the form of a spiritual director named Katherine DeGrow, a clergywoman living in the Dallas area. She heard my hunger and helped me name my longing. She validated my discomfort, not as a spiritual malady—something that was *wrong* with me—but as a call from God, something that was right on schedule. I will never forget her comforting words. "If the Spirit of God never nudged us or made us uncomfortable," she commented, "why would we ever let go of our old ways of doing things? How could we grow? God is simply calling you to a new kind of relationship."

"So what do I do now?" I asked Katherine. She had exposed my need to relinquish control of my spiritual journey to God. I thought I understood it now, but I was still in effort-mode. I was waiting for my next assignment—a list of disciplines and books and behaviors that could satisfy the hunger, fix my problem. But what Katherine gently and lovingly led me into was a major shift in my spiritual life—from active to passive, from controlling to allowing, from directing to participating, from trying harder to letting go.

At first, it seemed too simple. Okay, I get it; I can quit striving, quit trying so hard and allow God to work with me. Easy. I found, however, that control of my own spiritual process was deeply ingrained. And horror of horrors, I would have to stop analyzing and start listening. How does one *do* that? What would I do without my ladder list to spiritual health? How could I trust

God to direct my life? What if I had to do things I didn't want to do—contemporary equivalents of Old Testament sacrifices? Was I really being asked to surrender my agenda for my life? After all, I was the one who lived in this human skin of mine; I could just read the Bible and figure out what would be best and do it.

"Not so," she said. "It's time to let go of control."

Okay, I thought. I'll invite others to join me in this contemplative search. So, with the pastor's permission, I wrote a brief article in our church newsletter, inviting anyone interested in discussing contemplative prayer to meet with me the following week. We would form a lively discussion group, select a helpful book to study, and support each other in the search.

Not one person showed up. No one for this extrovert to engage in conversation. No one to intellectualize with me. No one to feed my addiction to striving. I felt alone, disappointed, and desperate. Which is of course exactly what I needed, if my journey had any chance of deepening. I was being invited to relinquish control of my spiritual life by opening myself to God in a new way, exploring the path toward contemplative prayer—in solitude. And that meant letting go of my usual methods.

The offering of myself as an empty (but willing) container was the toughest discipline I ever tried. True silence didn't come easily for me. It still doesn't, but there were teachers and companions along the way who helped me as a struggling novice to begin to experience, not just "know about," availability and emptiness. Nonetheless, there were no spiritual companions at first. I guess God knew that, given the warmth of another seeker, I would draw all my energy and inspiration from those around me and go galloping down some pathway to being a "better Christian." In this new contemplative aspect of the journey, my skills at organization were worthless.

As I entered the land of letting go, I found that, not only were my familiar coping tools inadequate, they actually *got in the way*. Letting go is not about gritting your teeth or putting your shoulder to the wheel or your nose to the grindstone. In other words, it's not about *trying harder*.

Though, let's face it, *trying* is our cultural action of first resort. The voices come seeping out of the woodwork, encouraging us to "pull ourselves up by our own bootstraps"; become the captains of our own ships; *make it happen*. Strength is measured by the amount of control we exert over our lives. Our ideas become obsessions. We seek security, certainty, and predictable outcomes.

You can do a PowerPoint proposal on your top ten career goals or schedule a PTA meeting on your Palm Pilot, but when it comes to your spiritual life, *this kind of management just won't work*. Jesus told us as much when he repeatedly pointed out the reversal of values in the kingdom of God. "The last shall be first . . ." he told his surprised listeners. "Whoever loses his life for my sake shall find it. . . ." He extolled the blessings of being meek and poor in spirit, of living in a posture of radical trust in God, all of which leads us toward a kind of spiritual releasing that feels counter-cultural to us.

The fact is that spiritual formation toward true freedom in Christ is:

- more about yielding than controlling,
- more about loosening than grasping,
- more about participating than directing,
- more about allowing than managing.

I could tell this was a territory of unfamiliar terrain and I would do well to explore its contours and detours. But above all, I had to give myself permission to let it happen, rather than make it happen—and to move at a snail's pace.

Letting Go Is a Complex Choice

As I began to engage in the letting-go process, I realized I was taking the first step in a very complex journey. Letting go is essentially saying *yes* to a process that is far from easy. It is full of ups and downs, stops and starts, and puzzling paradoxes. We venture forth, full of resolve—trying again—only to find ourselves back in our grasping mode, holding on to something for dear life, sometimes out of fear and sometimes out of familiarity. So we learn, slowly but surely, what it means to cooperate with the grace of God, to become partners with the Source who can guide us to wholeness.

Is it our work for God or God's work in us? The answer is yes, yes. We must enter the dance of being both active and passive, willing to do our part in action and effort, yet somehow respecting the work of the Spirit in and through us—a delicate balance indeed.

Letting Go Is a Courageous Choice

This process is not for the faint-hearted. Wading into this complex territory, full of spiritual challenges and emotional landmines, means confronting some of our own unhealed wounds and manipulative behavior patterns. In other words, we are faced with the need to be responsible for our own stuff! It is not only about letting go of "what they did to me," but honestly delving into our reasons for grasping. When we enter openly into God's formation of us, we uncover prejudices, faulty ideas, phony ways of relating, old resentments—a whole host of barriers to our capacity to let go. Understandably, we can be appalled and discouraged by this kind of self-knowledge. However, each tiny step forward brings the satisfying feeling of shedding baggage, creating a spiritual buoyancy that rewards us for staying the course.

A loving God leads us toward letting go as a *natural* process of the abundant life. It's our task to remove the blocks, to allow it to happen. Ultimately, we are even called to let go of letting go!

Letting Go Is a Continual Choice

In other words, the challenge keeps returning. We may think we have completed the work of letting go, only to have it resurface in another situation, wearing a different hat. And it nudges us, like a familiar friend, as if to say, "I'm baa-ack!"

Letting go is a continual choice that has to do with the peeling back of our layers of awareness. We may let go of a particular behavior only to discover the need to let go of the attitude or perspective underlying that behavior. For instance, if I'm attempting to let go of my need for the approval of others and uncover my own need to be liked, I'm apt to find that underneath lies a lack of confidence in who I am as a child of God. I am not in touch with the inner certainty that I am uniquely created, valued, loved, and forgiven by God. I have not experienced the still small voice whispering "You are my beloved." Too often our belief that God forgives (particularly us) is a matter of lip service, not a profound, inner *knowing*.

In *Life of the Beloved*, Henri Nouwen wrote of our tendency to allow other voices to drown out the forgiving voice of God—voices of culture and society. And the still small voice of God gets lost in the din.

> It was as if I kept refusing to hear the voice that speaks from the very depth of my being and says: "You are my Beloved, on you my favor rests." That voice has always been there, but it seems that I was much more eager to listen to other, louder voices saying: "Prove that you are worth something; do something relevant, spectacular or powerful, and then you will earn the love you so desire." Meanwhile, the soft, gentle voice that speaks in the silence remained unheard or, at least, unconvincing.[1]

At its spiritual depth, the process of letting go is a path to silencing those competing voices, clearing the barriers to our wholeness in God. When we experience that deep acceptance by God *as we are*, something within us shifts. We begin to believe that we are loved and forgiven offspring, treasured by the very Creator of the world. Others may be able to hurt us, disappoint us, disapprove of us, but they can no longer tell us who we are. They can't dislodge our core identity as God's beloved.

Letting Go Is a Compassionate Choice

Any decision to let go involves compassion for others and for ourselves. As we let go of resentments and grudges, compassion calls on us to forgive persons, not behaviors. After all, letting go is not condoning wrongdoing. It is releasing ourselves from the bondage and baggage of the angry feelings.

It is virtually impossible to be genuinely compassionate toward another without extending that same compassion to ourselves. As we uncover our self-deceptions and shortcomings, our *need* for mercy becomes more real to us. Our false pride dissolves. We accept the astounding forgiveness of God as a reality, not merely a grandiose idea, and we begin to see ourselves through God's compassionate eyes. It's a beautifully contagious process, allowing God's forgiveness to flow through our own lives and extending to others. Forgiveness can't be forced; it must be allowed.

So, letting go is not denial. Letting go is not condoning hurtful behavior. Letting go is not behavior modification. Letting go is not being "above it all." It is loosening our grip on attachments. It is a profound spiritual process that removes barriers to our true selves and our communion with God. It is making ourselves available to serve a marginalized and hurting world. It is entering into the process of loss and gain that literally shapes our lives here on earth and places us in harmony with creation as God ordained it.

In theory, we all yearn for this harmony. However, as we enter this land of letting go, we discover some uncharted detours and perilous ditches. Much will be required of us in terms of courage, persistence, and willingness to change course. But just hold on. The tunnels may be dark and the ride may be bumpy, but it's the road to *freedom*.

For Reflection

1. Have you ever felt a "hunger for God"? How does the hunger manifest itself?

2. What seems to cause your spiritual restlessness? What are your usual ways of quelling that sense of dis-ease?

3. Describe a time when you have felt the "nudge" of God. What change, if any, resulted from it?

4. What changes would you need to make to release more control of your own spiritual process to God?

Part II
Letting Go—of What?

The signs of bondage were evident—the swinging foot, the darting eyes, the clasping and unclasping of her hands. Clara's body was shouting "Anxiety" and "Discontent." There were less obvious clues, too—a sluggish hesitation in her speech, long sighs before replying, a dismissive shrug of the shoulders, a distant sadness underlying her clever comments.

Clara remarked (with yet another sigh), "I'm sure I need to 'let go and let God,' but I can't seem to get going with it." She was wound up as tightly as a brand new ball of yarn.

Part of Clara's difficulty—and our own—was coming to the process of letting go in strokes writ large, generalities with no specifics, idealistic goals with no flesh-and-blood connection. In short, it's unlikely that any of us can let go unless we know what we're clinging to. And that "ball of yarn" has be to unraveled, one thread at a time. Do you need to let go of a relationship? A habit? A way of thinking? The following pages will offer a few sample threads for your consideration.

Letting Go of People

I am about to do a new thing; . . . do you not perceive it? (Isa 43:19)

. . . all things work together for good for those who love God . . . (Rom 8:28)

One of the toughest challenges in life is maintaining our equilibrium when we lose a person dear to us through divorce or death, through choice or chance. The pang of loss has countless origins. An adult child may move far, far away to pursue a dream; a friendship may fade as interests diverge; a betrayal may burn the bridges of trust. Loss of relationship hurts.

There's a poignant story of a little boy who woke up in the middle of the night, terrified by a scary nightmare. His cries of distress brought his father quickly to his bedside with words of comfort. "There, there, Johnny, it's okay, son. Remember you're never alone; God is always here and God loves you." With childlike candor, Johnny replied, "But, Daddy, sometimes I need someone with *skin* on!"

Like Johnny, as human beings we yearn for divine comfort in the form of flesh-and-blood people, and it comes to us through friends, family, and other personal relationships. Because they bring so much sustenance and joy to our lives, it's no wonder we try to hold on to them for dear life.

But one day we must start to loosen our grip. Inability to release relationships can paralyze our growth, creating invisible barriers that block us at every turn. Sometimes we simply yearn for things to be the way they used to be. I recall the day a very wise counselor listened to my longing to get back to "normal," as I tried to deal with a loss.

"I just want to feel better," I cried. "Please tell me when I'll get over this!"

She replied very gently, "And who told you that was possible?"

I was horrified. I saw a life of continual sadness looming before me. But then the counselor began to explain the process of integrating a loss, of making it part of the fiber of my being, allowing the healing that would bring hidden gifts out of the experience. Believe me, it's possible. Our task is, by the grace of God, to pick up the shredded pieces of our lives and somehow re-weave the threads. The fabric won't be exactly the same, but it can still form a beautiful pattern, albeit a different one.

Once we have confronted the truth of our feelings, whether they be angry, amiable, or sad, we can find constructive ways to honor the gifts of the lost relationship, let go of the hurts, and move on.

Death and Divorce

Death

To say that the death of a spouse is devastating seems painfully trite in its understatement. Though there is a treasure-trove of helpful literature available on this subject, I learned of its turbulent variations first-hand from a friend who suffered two losses in her immediate family within five years. The tragedies rearranged the pieces of her world.

Janie suffered the shocking death of her robust fifty-year-old husband, Harry, from a surprise heart attack. One moment, he was waving goodbye as he left for the office, the next moment she received the call that he was dead. They had been sweethearts since their teenage years, marrying young, and had survived the accidental death of their twenty-five-year-old daughter, Anne, only three years earlier.

I remember her attempt at describing her feelings: "There are really no words," she said, "just a feeling of amputation as if living parts of me had been suddenly cut away, with no warning and no anesthesia."

The journey from fragmentation to wholeness was painful and slow, one moment at a time, almost one cell at a time. Since both of the losses had been sudden, the shock effect took an enormous toll. It was a long time before any signs of healing began to emerge, when Janie could even begin to see herself as separate from Anne and Harry. She went back to work, functioning like a robot, appearing confident and all together. But inside she was on a roller-coaster ride of emotions—and she was not the driver. She was bandied about by emotional extremes of anger, love, loneliness, guilt, hope. After several months she found herself at a church meeting with friends, smiling for the first time, laughing at someone's witty remarks. She left the gathering with the ebullient hope that she would be able to smile again. But, only minutes later, her hopes were dashed. As she entered her empty house, she surprisingly collapsed into a pit of despair deeper than she had ever known.

Praying in any conventional sense seemed impossible. She experienced instead what felt like a kind of dialogue with both her husband and her daughter, saying all that had been left unsaid and feeling that she had been heard. This instinctive reaching out into the Mystery led her to the Source of All, and she became even more deeply rooted in God. Her firm belief in life after death opened the way for a feeling of intense connection to her loved ones.

She began to notice that God's grace and comfort arrived in unexpected packages—mostly from those who had walked before her into widowhood. After a traumatic first Christmas with her in-laws soon after Harry's death, an eighty-year-old neighbor paid Janie a visit to see how she had fared during the holidays. When Janie described the Christmas dinner, where the atmosphere was suffocating with pain, the neighbor, Cora, remarked, "It wasn't the same, was it? I mean, they treated you differently, didn't they, as if you were to blame somehow." The words were stinging in their honesty, but strangely comforting. Janie realized someone had gently placed words on her feelings of hurt and bewilderment. At any family gathering in those first months, there was simply more agony in one room than anyone could bear. She was able to identify the subtle effects of our human tendency to assign blame, an unspoken feeling within the family circle that someone had to be responsible for such searing pain. Cora's words of understanding were like a healing balm to her.

With the perspective and passage of seven years since the second of those tragic deaths, I asked Janie to reflect on what had aided her in the letting-go process. She revealed that part of her healing had come through attending to her own journey into wholeness. As she put one foot in front of the other, first in mere survival, then slowly gaining strength, she began to feel less fragmented, less dependent on others.

But, she admitted, she didn't always experience forward motion. Some days brought indescribable turmoil, feelings of desperation and hopelessness. She was frightened by the new vulnerability that enveloped her, a realization that everything, *everything*, was subject to loss. Safety was indeed an illusion. But with that loss of innocence, there was a growing acceptance that she could never get Harry and Anne back. She could love her husband and daughter dearly, honor and appreciate their gifts to her life, but find her deepest identity in a God who would never leave her. She found herself stronger in the broken places, like a tree whose roots had gained strength from the storm.

And she glimpsed a horizon of hope.

Divorce

Recovery from divorce has some distinct differences from the death of a spouse. The two experiences have often been contrasted using the metaphor of the sword. Death makes a final, clean cut; divorce carries a jagged edge. In either case, the loss is life-altering.

To be sure, there are times when two people arrive at a mutual decision to part with no residual rancor. They may have exhausted every effort, from counseling to prayer, before deciding that divorce is the path to follow. Under those circumstances, it may be less painful to let go of the relationship without continuing the damage. In most instances, however, divorce produces feelings of profound failure surrounded by anger, resentment, and guilt. Those affected by divorce must let go not only of the relationship itself, but also the accompanying feelings of rage, remorse, regret, or rejection. The experience is so wrenching that in order to salvage meaning from it, it's important to extract every single lesson possible. Otherwise, the emotional waste is overwhelming and unbearable. At the least, a broken relationship provides an opportunity to honestly explore what went awry so that each person can somehow grow from that knowledge.

But before the lessons can be uncovered and faced, one must first withdraw focus from the wrongdoing of the other person. In other words, quit the blame game. One must have the courage to take a piercing look at the situation and ask, "What can I glean from this?" Blame is easier, of course, but it diverts and obscures the lessons.

Our culture sets up some pretty imposing stumbling blocks to the success of marriage, producing a whole range of unrealistic expectations. I was part of a generation reared on fairytale endings and syrupy romantic ballads. Most of our ideas of love were shaped by Cinderella stories and Doris Day movies. Music like "Embraceable You" and "You're My Everything" formed our relational expectations just as hymns like "The Old Rugged Cross" and "Washed in the Blood" formed our theology.

"They lived happily every after" seemed not only something we could attain, but something we deserved. Somehow we absorbed the notion that marriage partners were to be perpetually kind, constantly nurturing, each in a state of self-denial for the benefit of the other—surely a recipe for disappointment and disaster. True love was seen as a feeling by which one was overwhelmed, rather than a mature, thoughtful process to which one was committed. Unfortunately, the common tendency to confuse *real* love with *feelings* of love paves the way for people to engage in unbridled self-deception and mistake that for the truth.

In many cases, couples can face their adolescent ideas about love *together*, working in concert to "grow up" into a mature love relationship. All too frequently, however, a divorce ensues instead, leaving a trail of unimaginable heartbreak in its wake.

The jagged edge in the experience of divorce involves an ongoing set of emotional lacerations—feeling replaced as you see your spouse with someone else, losing your place in your spouse's extended family, and watching innocent children suffer undeserved feelings of abandonment. And that's only the beginning of the scenario that continues for years. How is it possible to let all that go?

In my own experience, I discovered that forgiveness and acceptance aren't solely acts of benevolence and altruism. I wanted to *live* life, not merely *survive* it. And to do that, I needed to let go of a ton of negative baggage. The core motivation to start letting it all go is profound self-interest.

I remember that long-ago moment when I knew I had to do it. As a newly divorced forty-year-old woman, I was out for the evening with some new women friends who were also divorced. After I returned home, the conversations started replaying in my mind. We had been talking about the rottenness of our situations—how tough it was, how lonely it was, how callously we had been tossed aside. The bitterness was growing like poison ivy, spreading its toxic roots into our faces, our words, our view of life. We piously called on God more as an avenger of our honor than the ground of our hope.

No matter how justified the negative feelings might be, I knew I didn't want to *live* there. Letting go is first a matter of awareness, then of desire to enter the process. As I became aware of the insidious bitterness that was creeping into my life, I was horrified at what was happening to me. I promised myself I would try to monitor my thoughts and words, weeding out the negativism whenever possible. However, I found that my most sincere intentions often went down the path of resentment and snide remarks, and I had to begin all over again.

Sometimes I became so doggedly cheerful that my demeanor was little more than behavior modification, as a voice inside my head urged me to keep smiling, keep pretending everything was fine. Delicate discernment was finally necessary to emphasize the positive without suppressing the negative. I didn't always achieve that balance. In my effort to look on the bright side of things, I often failed to provide a safe place for legitimate grief—my own grief and that of others.

The letting go wasn't a once-for-all-time action. I had to deal with one thought at a time, one event at a time, using all the spiritual resources I had in my storehouse at the pivotal age of forty. For years, the jagged edge continued to lacerate, threatening to open the deep wounds again. To be honest, I still encounter subtle stumbling blocks on the road to letting go every day of my life. I can't be a perfect survivor any more than I can be a perfect person. There is always a persistent inclination to remain in our woundedness in the past rather than pursue the healing that can occur only in the present. However, the more we cling to our hurts, the more our present and future will reflect the life of a victim.

For me, it was difficult to learn the difference between suppressing an emotion and releasing it. I'm still not sure I'm skilled at drawing a sharp distinction, but I know there is one. My tendency to don my "steel magnolia" persona, gritting my teeth and resolving "not to think about it," only caused the emotional pain to go underground, seeking a hidden psychic space in which to fester its poison. Through years of trial and error, I began to learn to feel the emotion, express it without attacking or hurting anyone, and release it, using whatever techniques were at my disposal. (These will be discussed in Part III). I learned that there is no such thing as a "bad feeling." Feelings simply are. They have something to teach us. What we choose to do with them is another matter.

Letting go of people who have been important in our lives certainly involves more than alleviating pain. It helps to affirm every single positive aspect we can recall about the person and the relationship, returning to those thoughts repeatedly as we move forward and begin to honor the good stuff.

Even if a marriage has failed, there may be children to be cherished and memories to be treasured. We must separate the flowers from the weeds, pressing the flowers in a scrapbook of sorts and allowing the weeds to die.

Therefore, no matter who did what, no matter how things went awry, the moment comes when it's time to move on. Not to do so is to poison your very being. The clever adage is all too true: "Resentment hurts the vessel in which it is stored more than the object on which it is poured."

Letting Go of Our Children

Train children in the right way, and when old, they will not stray. (Prov 22:6)

I knew that letting go of a teenager could be a risky business, but my eager resolve to do so was graphically tested one spring night in Texas. I was sleeping soundly when the telephone jolted me awake, and a familiar voice whispered, "Mom, remember The Pact?" Even though the covenant had been forged more than a year before, I definitely remembered it.

My eighteen-year-old son Harrison and I had made the agreement the previous year following a series of troubling teen suicides in the Dallas area where we were living at the time. There had been newspaper stories of the young people who had taken their own lives rather than risk embarrassing their parents by confessing involvement in questionable activities. Harrison and I had read the newspapers and shared the grief of the whole community as everyone tried to make sense of the tragedies. As we talked about the power of parental disappointment, I assured him that I cared more about his *life* than about his good behavior. So The Pact was born. We devised a plan we hoped would provide a safety net when and if he found himself in a jam.

These were the terms of The Pact: Should he ever find himself in a compromising or dangerous situation of any kind, he was to call me *pronto*. I promised to come to get him—no questions asked. At first he was incredulous that I would act on his behalf with no explanation whatsoever. I vowed to uphold my end of the bargain, but my insides were quivering with uncertainty. Sure it was risky, but I felt that drastic measures were necessary to convince him that I meant what I said. We hugged on it, and that had been that—until that telephone rang.

Harrison quickly told me where he was—a Holiday Inn on a busy Dallas freeway. In a flash, I covered my nightgown with a raincoat and sped off to the rescue, my heart pounding with alarm. I saw the blinking blue lights of police cars long before I saw the Holiday Inn marquee. As I entered the confusion, I spotted a lone figure standing under a tree in the dark corner of the parking lot. I knew it was Harrison. He silently got into the car and we headed toward home. For a while, neither of us said a single word. Then I heard a deep sigh, followed by a trembling young voice, "Oh, heck, Mom, I might as well tell you about it."

Friends had picked him up at our home for a routine school party, or so it began. However, an after-party party ensued, moving the merriment to the

Holiday Inn. Some of the group began drinking and the noise level escalated to the point of disturbance. When the management confronted the teenagers about their rowdiness and threatened to call the police, Harrison smelled trouble and, thankfully, sneaked off to call me.

Under the conditions of The Pact, he was under no obligation to tell me what had happened, and I like to believe that I would have honored his silence. In fact, like any parent, there were countless times when I longed to know the details of my sons' struggles and had to bite my tongue to allow them some shred of independence and privacy. Of course, there were other times when my need for control got the best of me and I pressed relentlessly for privileged information.

But that particular night, Harrison and I were keenly aware of the perils of the letting-go process and the costly lessons for both of us. And we were deeply grateful for The Pact.

In another parental agreement during my sons' teen years, there were understandable ups and downs, but in retrospect this agreement, too, was worth the risk. After hearing a number of colorful stories about the foolhardy antics of college freshmen, I was anticipating my sons' first year of independence with some anxiety. It seemed that the kids who acted most outrageously when they left home were the ones who had been most closely supervised during the teen years. It was as if they had had no practice at assuming responsibility for their own lives. I wanted my sons to experience what it feels like to be *trusted*, to get a taste of that kind of empowerment.

With that in mind, I had a talk with each of the boys at the beginning of their senior year in high school, reminding them that in a mere twelve months, they would be away in another city, making their own choices about where to go, when to study, whom to befriend, when to come home, and how to behave. We talked about the need for practice in learning any skill—from riding a bike to playing the piano. And we decided on a sort of "dress rehearsal" for their college years.

The rules were these: they would be responsible for telling me where they were going, with whom, for what, and when they would be home. I was going out on a limb to trust their judgment as they "practiced" the art of self-governance. In the event their evening plans changed, they were to call and let me know. If they abused the agreement by irresponsible actions, the deal was off.

The "trial" year was not a bed of roses. There were tense moments when I questioned the wisdom of what I had done. But it was worth it. At least the boys' initial struggles at independence occurred at home rather than on the college campus. In their words, "By the time I got to college, making my own decisions was *no big deal!*" We all must find ways to support our children's independence, ways to affirm their best decision-making powers, from the choice of what shirt to wear to what job to take. And no, they won't always make wise choices, and neither will we.

Our children often suffer from our own compulsions to control them. We tell ourselves we're simply trying to protect them from harm, but I suspect that some of our actions mask our own need to be needed by our children. We have a hidden yearning to be rescuers, protectors, the ones with the answers to life's dilemmas, the ones who can keep them from the teacher's anger, the family's disapproval, the banker's summons, and the dangers of an unfriendly environment.

But it's more insidious and unconscious than that. It's understandable that we want to be in close relationship with our children, but this apparently desirable emotion carries a hidden shadow that can escape our understanding. At the time of my divorce, a wise pediatrician tried to warn me of the dangers of exposing my sons to the pain I was going through. His years of experience had taught him that when a parent's pain is shared with a child as confidante, the child will automatically move into a comforter-role unsuitable for his tender age. I was urged to lean on the support of caring friends rather than expect my sons to fill the relational vacuum in my life. Though it was inevitable that they witnessed my struggle with the pain and loss, it wasn't their responsibility to make it better. I did a reasonably good job of refraining from overt negative statements about their father and his new life, but my unconscious neediness was a magnet that pulled them into my emotional pain. Unfortunately, I didn't realize my sensitive older son was sometimes engulfed in this toxic role of "parenting the parent," and the damage to him has taken a long time to heal.

We all have empty places inside us needing to be loved, and the unconditional love of a child is drawn to the vacuum. It's necessary to be keenly aware of our own neediness so that we can refrain from using children in these inappropriate ways. It becomes so easy to use their devotion to satisfy our own unconscious needs that we rarely notice our subtle motives, even when it erupts in rebellion years later.

With the wisdom of hindsight and experience, I see now that one of our goals as parents should be to hear our children say one day, "She loves us, but her happiness is not dependent on what we do." Perhaps one of the greatest gifts we can give our children is a life of our own.

Letting go of children begins the moment they toddle away from us on two wobbly legs, and it never ends. We send them off to day care, to first grade, to college, to marriage. However, the subtle need to let go of emotional control, with all its guilt-producing manipulations, calls for loving maturity on our part. We will always be groping for the balance between giving too much (having too few boundaries) and giving too little (boundaries that feel like abandonment). Dig a little deeper and we encounter the letting go of our role as full-time parents and the necessity of forging a new relationship with our adult children. And beneath that, still another layer calls for an authentic trust in a loving God as we launch them out into the world.

We all struggle to locate that fine line between concern and control. Even now, even though I *know better*, I sometimes can't resist the maternal urge to "make it all right" for my kids. There are times when, even in the face of every rational argument against it, my need to rescue still has the power to trump the need to let go. I've said it before and I'll say it again: this letting-go stuff is no cake-walk.

Friendship

> No one has greater love than this, to lay down one's life for one's friends.
> (John 15:13)

We are born into our families, but we choose our friends. And like the proverbial balm in Gilead, they "soothe our souls," often filling in the painful gaps left unfulfilled in other personal attachments. The jack-of-all-trades in the relationship category, friendship presents a unique dilemma when it's time to let go.

George Santayana's writings on the categories of friendship show the depth of their diversity. He wrote that "friendship is always the union of a part of one mind with a part of another; we are friends in 'spots.'"[1]

I tried in vain to find a working definition of friendship. Webster's Dictionary notwithstanding, I imagine that everyone defines friendship in terms of their own experience of it. Like many matters of the heart, it reveals a great deal about our own unconscious needs, as we naturally reach out for others to fill a void in ourselves.

We have convenience friends, whose lives routinely intersect with ours. We have special-interest friends with whom we share a particular activity. We have historical friends, who knew us way back when. We have crossroads friends who shared a life event with us. We have cross-generational friends, where the wisdom of one generation enlivens the other. And, if we're lucky, we have close friends, whose special bond transcends time and space—friends we can call at three in the morning.

Other categories I'd add to Santayana's list are family friends (not friends *of* the family, but friends *in* the family), spiritual friends who help us along our spiritual journey, and soul friends with whom we have a mysterious connection for no discernible reason.

Sometimes friendships simply run their course, and the relationship tends to deteriorate if it becomes forced. Perhaps the mutual interests that once couldn't be exhausted in three days now can fill only three minutes. Perhaps the common thread that once held you together has become frayed. Perhaps the tennis game you once enjoyed together now gives you a bum knee. Perhaps you've discovered that being with that friend now absolutely depletes your energy.

I once had a delightful friend in another city who was what might be humorously labeled a shopaholic. Our time together would invariably end at some posh shopping mall as she indulged her addiction with the blessing of her generous and wealthy husband. Though I valued her company, I began to see that the friendship was not bringing out the best in me as I lugged home bulging bags of stuff I didn't need. I made a choice to spend less time with her and to steer our meetings toward safer venues. We remained dear friends, but in a different context.

There are many illusions to which we cling in this relational realm. For instance, we tend to think of solid friends as those who will stand by us in tough times. The truth is that it's often easier to console our friends than to congratulate them. To rush to a friend's side during a crisis awakens our need to be needed. Not so when that friend has occasion to rejoice. For example, when your son has just been rejected by the local state college, it may be difficult to celebrate with a friend whose son has received a Harvard scholarship. When you can't have children of your own, it's an enormous act of generosity to knit a baby blanket for a friend's newborn. Friendship has its challenges as well as its delights.

Friends can't be all things to us. Friendships can't be perfect. Releasing our illusions about friendships can open the way to appreciating the richness of their imperfections. We must allow the relationship to evolve and change.

Letting go of a friendship often *feels* as if there is a lack of love and loyalty— that the demise of the friendship is someone's fault. There are simply times when it seems prudent to honor a friendship for what it was, and let it go.

For Reflection

1. Think of a time when others have been "God with skin on" in your life. What did they do that nurtured you? Are there people in your life to whom you could minister in the same way?

2. How do you process emotional upheaval? Do you talk about your feelings rather than feeling them?

3. What relationship in your circle of family and friends needs healing or letting go of hurts?

Letting Go of Personas

For those who want to save their life will lose it, and those who lose their life for my sake will find it. (Matt 16:25)

Michelangelo was once asked how he created his incredible sculptures, teeming with soulful beauty. He replied that the statue already existed within the marble; he simply chipped away the excess marble and allowed God's creation to be.

So it is with us. In the process of letting go, we chip away the bits of our false, adaptive selves that obscure the human work of art at the heart of us, miraculously crafted in God's image.

And just how do these false layers accumulate? One insidious, unconscious drop at a time. In short, we learn how to survive in our culture. We repeat behaviors that get us what we want, that please those whose approval we seek, that fit into conventional society. Through years of adaptation, we become identified with those behaviors and say, "This is who I am," not bothering to question their authenticity.

So the masks and roles accumulate, layer upon layer. Some may be life-enhancing, honest extensions of our true selves. And others may simply be familiar, even manipulative, and not really connected to our essence. The trick is to discern thoughtfully what truly fits within us and what doesn't. Only then can we make a decision about whether to let it go. Awareness must precede action. We must summon the courage to look honestly at the personas we're clutching and *why*.

In unraveling some of the personas we present to the world, it may be helpful to distinguish between roles and masks. Roles refer to the legitimate undertakings of our personhood—daughter, son, mother, husband, community leader, caretaker—personas of which we are usually conscious. Masks, on the other hand, typically involve ways we present ourselves that may not be authentic to our nature. We may not even be aware that we're wearing them. But to get along in the world, we learn early how to adapt to what *works*.

Volumes have been written about the masks women wear. We're the "steel magnolias" who can cushion everyone's feelings; we can unravel emotional entanglements within the family; we'll take the chicken wing instead of the breast. Life becomes a series of tasks to be accomplished, days to be endured. We keep saying "yes," to requests, then complaining that "they" are putting too much on us. We may do good things, but we make sure that somehow everyone knows how hard we've worked and sacrificed and how tired we are—clear indicators of the martyr mask.

Our culture offers masks for men also—the stoic Marlboro men, marching on the frontiers of life, slaying the dragons, rescuing the damsel in distress, pulling themselves up by their own bootstraps. A man receives applause for being the corporate workaholic, the rigid disciplinarian, the good provider, the financial wizard. Never doubt yourself, never give up, never cry—he is told. Be successful; the man with the most toys wins. And the real self, including the vulnerable side, often stays hidden behind a tough-guy façade.

Much of the process of letting go is a stripping away of layers of conditioning that obscure our true nature, layers that reflect messages from our culture, parents, and authority figures, as well as our own unconscious survival techniques. Each person has a unique set of masks. The only ones with which I'm deeply familiar are a few I've been able to identify (so far!) in my own life. Perhaps you'll be led to formulate and examine your own personal list.

Masks

> Even though our outer nature is wasting away, our inner nature is being renewed day by day. (2 Cor 4:16)

The Martyr

In my family of origin, the women were schooled to be long-suffering caretakers of the men and children, in that order. To be worthwhile meant to put your needs last, to sacrifice willingly for others. Everyday comments carried an unspoken message of approval and rewarded the martyr-mask: "She works her fingers to the bone." "She always puts her family first." "She never rests." "She's so unselfish." I inadvertently assumed the mantle of the women who preceded me, believing it was a worthy mask to put on.

I remember the day I reluctantly became aware of my martyr mask—the one that projects dogged duty at all costs, a self-effacing efficiency accomplished through gritted teeth. My then-teenage sons were paying the price for this masquerade, and one day their banter exposed the martyr mask.

The time was early evening, that familiar family rush hour when everything converges at five o'clock—dinner preparation, homework, and the race against time for a variety of seven o'clock meetings. As I dashed around the kitchen, slamming cabinet doors and calling out instructions, Harrison gently elbowed David and said knowingly, "She's doing it again."

Barely overhearing his stage whisper, I demanded to know what he meant. Silently, I was fuming. "How *could* they be so critical and sassy, after all the things I do for them?!" As I pushed for an explanation, they began to back-pedal and stonewall to cover their tracks, but I would have none of it. Finally, Harrison explained with a sigh, "Mom, every time you have too much on your plate and get into such a snit, you have a way of *poisoning* the atmosphere around here!"

My angry reaction was suddenly blunted by an inner awareness that I needed to pay attention. Suppressing my defensiveness, I said, "I don't know what you mean. . . . Explain this to me." And to my dismay, they did.

They pantomimed my jerky body language, mimicked the tone of my voice, and portrayed the picture of a duty-driven woman whose anxiety and resentment were contagious. With uncharacteristic humility I said, "I don't want to be this way. Please help me change this."

The boys explained that they could see it coming long before it erupted. They could sense the build-up, though I was largely unaware of it. It had become such a familiar mask that I couldn't see it coming. So after much discussion, we arrived at a plan that would preclude any verbal confrontation. When either of them sensed the hectic pattern on the horizon, he would gently hold up a "stop" hand in front of my face, alerting me to the situation with no words spoken by either of us. Then the response would be up to me.

During the weeks that followed, I was humbled by the degree to which I was unconscious of my behavior. Time after time, I was surprised by a hand rising in front of my face, and I slowly made progress toward awareness. I could let go of this toxic mask only as I faced it honestly and willingly.

My children have been great teachers—as you'll see in the pages ahead. To this day, some twenty-five years later, when my frustration begins to build, and the martyr mask overtakes me, an invisible hand seems to appear in front of my face.

The Good Girl

The prevailing slogans of my childhood carried powerful messages within their cutesy lingo: "Pretty is as pretty does," and "You catch more flies with honey than vinegar." In other words, get what you want and need by being charming, not straightforward. My unspoken and unconscious posture became: "Tell me what you want me to be, and I will be just that."

It was a world in which pleasing behavior was rewarded by adult approval and peer popularity, where well-mannered girls were encouraged to look good and act good, to appear poised on the outside and disregard the chaos on the inside. And above all, we were taught to keep smiling.

I soon learned to get in line with this persona, to move toward being compliant, conforming, and *sweet*. The young women of my generation were encouraged (usually nonverbally) to hide unpleasant feelings and bite their lips to conceal controversial opinions. Most of the time, I willingly deferred to the men in my relational orbit. Over the years, like most everyone else, I instinctively adapted to what worked. Not only did I think it was the most effective way to live, I thought it was the *right* way, the Christian way. I had no idea it was a mask. Rather, it seemed a proper reflection of the way things "ought" to be.

Superwoman

No task is too great, no tragedy too terrible to bear; she will rise to the occasion, no matter the cost to herself. Fatigue is not in her vocabulary! This mask creates the illusion of an unapproachable, un*real* person—a woman with no visible warts or weaknesses. As one who is unable to acknowledge her own pain, she is disconnected from the pain of others at an emotional level, even while performing her endless acts of ministry.

When we keep up a façade of constant competence, not only do we ultimately exhaust our own resources, but we also create a wall of separation that makes it difficult for others to share their vulnerability with us. Think about it. Are you inclined to share your doubts and fears with someone who doesn't seem to have any?

Victim

This is one persona that deserves a category all its own. The victim mask is understandable on the one hand and insidious on the other. We need to become aware of its shadow side, which can sneak up on us without detection.

Now don't get me wrong; I'm not talking about suppression of legitimate emotion. When we've been hurt by the actions of others, the pain is real and visceral and needs an outlet. We need time to feel it, rail against it, call for justice when possible, and bring it to consciousness.

However, there is a subtle seduction to the role of victim that can stop our growth dead in its tracks. When the victim begins to identify with that role as *who he or she is*, then being a victim becomes a perverse badge of honor, worn unconsciously to engender sympathy or procure aid. Unfortunately, some folks cling to that persona even after years of expensive therapy. Though it makes me cringe to admit it, we seem to have an unconscious ego investment in suffering.

The victim mask is worn by women and men alike. I know a man who has good health, a successful business, money and the time to spend it, and plenty of loving friends—in short, an enviable life. Yet when you ask him how he's doing, he recites a litany of complaints about every aspect of his life, as if he is searching every hidden corner for negative material. "Receipts are down at work." "I'm tired all the time." "No one seems to have any time to talk anymore." And what's more, playing the role of victim has become such a habit that he is totally unaware of the gray aura that surrounds him.

Shedding the victim role means accepting what has happened to us. This doesn't mean we justify or condone it. It merely means that we cease judging it—over and over and over again. This allows us to participate in the reality of Rom 8:28: "All things work together for good for those who love God." Not all things *are* good, but rather all things can work together for our good, when we allow God to lead us toward growth. No matter how shattered our lives and no matter how they got that way, God works with us to pick up the broken pieces and refashion a life, using those pieces in a creative living mosaic. In order to grow, we may need to acknowledge the part we played in the situation—which may be a sobering and humbling realization. But as we let go of that rigid measuring stick called "fairness" and move toward the flexible one called "forgiveness," our attachment to the victim mask begins to loosen.

Roles

Most of the roles we play are necessary and legitimate. But we all know how easily we can lose our deepest essence as our identities become enmeshed in the lives of others. We begin to define ourselves as someone's wife or husband, someone's daughter or son, someone's mother or father. It becomes who we *are*. Then, when the need for that role disappears, it feels as if we ourselves disappear. In our own eyes, we cease to exist.

I reveled in the roles of wife and mother. Cooking, hosting family gatherings, being closely involved in the lives of a large contingent of friends, and most of all, being a mother to two sons, were roles that seemed to fit me. I delighted in them.

When my traumatic divorce rearranged the pieces of my life, I was frantically trying to reconstruct my persona, with limited success. Though I didn't realize it at the time, the loss of my identity as a married woman was just as shattering as the loss of the relationship. No longer a wife, I showered an inordinate amount of attention and affection on my sons, then ten and fifteen years old, in an unconscious attempt to fill the relational vacuum. Thank God they weren't completely smothered.

As I prayed for strength and guidance, I was unprepared for the surprising ways God would answer my pleas. In retrospect, it was part of a pattern I began to recognize through the years: every time I admitted my utter dependence on God's grace and opened my heart in a radical, agenda-less way, some unexpected invitation to newness would come out of left field.

This time it came in the person of an eccentric and talented theatre director in our small community. I barely knew Joe and was surprised to hear his voice on the phone. He was casting the musical *Mame* and desperately needed two young actors for the roles of young Patrick (about age ten to twelve) and older Patrick (seventeen to twenty). Since David and Harrison had the visual similarities of most siblings and could carry a tune, Joe wanted them at the auditions.

They reluctantly showed up and won the roles, hands down. But there was another surprise; Joe wanted to cast me as Mame. Since I had done little but sing in the church choir for fifteen years and had no significant theatre experience, it seemed an impossible task. He assured me that he would teach me the songs, teach me to dance and act, mold me into Mame. But the irresistible allure for me was the opportunity to work side by side with my sons on a project that would distract us from the fresh pain of the divorce.

And it did. Night after night, scene after scene, song after song, we immersed ourselves in the demanding pace of the production. I felt inept and clumsy, so accustomed to my narrow good-girl mask that I balked at risqué lines and flamboyant theatrics. Through the weeks, Joe competently chipped away at my woodenness and cajoled me out of my self-consciousness. I remember his prophetic words (which I rejected at the time): "Linda, a part of you *is* Mame, and you don't even know it!"

I kept clinging to my role as buttoned-up church lady and continued to view the play as simply a temporary project, one that might bring the boys and me closer as a family. But on opening night, as I took the last curtain call and joined the rest of the cast on stage, we knew that something had shifted. My sons' image of me as cookie-baker and carpool cabbie had taken on a new dimension. A role in a play had invited me to step from a traditional woman's role into a broader role as a person. The experience introduced me to a part of myself that I had never met.

I have learned something new every time life's roles begin to shift. As my sons grew older and the empty nest approached, another dormant layer of selfhood was ready to be discovered. Moving to a new city unleashed my familiar moorings and hastened the process.

I was a newcomer to Dallas after living my entire life in west Tennessee. The truth was, I had the enviable opportunity to fashion a new life, but it didn't feel enviable. Instead, I felt disconnected, uncentered, rootless—those unsettling emotions that stem from a loss of identity. I was in Big D, a big city full of electric vitality and endless activity. No one was expecting anything of me. No one recognized me in the grocery store. There were no pressing demands on my time. No one really knew me.

The good news was that there was a virtual banquet of tempting options, an opportunity (as my friends enviously told me) "to do all the things you've always wanted to do." The bad news was that I didn't have a clue to what I *wanted*. Like most women of my generation, I had derived my identity from what I thought *others* wanted from me. I'd never seriously asked myself the question: what do you really want? As a Christian, I'd been taught that the question itself was undeniably selfish and automatically outside the will of God.

My older son, then a student at Southern Methodist University, was the messenger for the words I needed to hear. As we grabbed a quick lunch between his classes one day, I was expressing my confusion and frustration about discovering God's will for me at this new stage of my life. With a look of exasperation, David heaved a sigh and put down his fork. His words were like a wake-up call. "Mom, who told you that God's will for you was always something that would make you suffer? Did you ever dare to think that God sometimes speaks to us through our gifts and delights, too? That's part of the Good News!"

His youthful trust spurred me into a time of discernment and openness that helped me explore not only the service projects I felt were worthwhile, but also those that sparked my sense of aliveness. I was ready for a new role, and the search for it expanded my perception of how God guides us toward newness.

Saints through the ages have testified to the joy of daring to believe that God wants us to use the gifts we've been given, to pursue the passionate interests that compel us, to be all that we are created to be. Frederick Buechner's famous words have guided many to lose their fear of trusting in a benevolent God. He counsels that your purpose is the place where your deep gladness meets the world's needs.

In other words, be willing to let go of your image of God as punitive schoolmaster who demands something out of harmony with your own soul. Jesus was equally incredulous at our tendency to look at God this way, as he exclaimed, "Is there anyone among you who, if your child asks for bread, will give a stone?" (Matt 7:9) Many of us, however, are reluctant to do the inner work necessary to know ourselves as God knows us, and thus to see ourselves as God sees us. Once we do, as we open ourselves to divine guidance, we will begin to sense opportunities where our passions intersect with the needs of those around us. You can count on it.

As we act out the ever-changing roles of our lives—son, daughter, mother, father, caretaker, breadwinner, grandparent—we're invited to meet the parts of our true selves revealed by those experiences, learning to distinguish what is a part of the role and what is authentically *us*. Our task is to hold those roles lightly, wearing them like pieces of clothing, something we don temporarily, allowing them to come and go. All too often, however, the role *becomes* who we are. Then when the role is no longer necessary, we feel emptied of our identity.

After years of being essentially defined by the lives, demands, and needs of others, it is frightening to knock at the door of your heart and wonder *who* is there! Men usually become identified by their work roles and women by their relational roles. A surgeon friend who kept postponing his retirement remarked to me one day, "I can't retire! If I did, then I wouldn't *be* anyone!" This should be a wake-up call for those who cannot adjust when an old role slips away.

What masks and roles govern your life? Your prevalent personas may be that of being the jokester, the rescuer, the know-it-all, the dummy, the beauty. Even if elements of the mask you wear are authentic, the mask represents only a portion of yourself at best. At its worst, it may distort your true nature.

Through the years, all of us assume masks that may seem to serve us in the short run. But, over the long haul, the true self becomes like an orphaned child—unknown, unloved, and unnurtured—hiding beneath our layers of costuming.

We must let go of who we thought we were so that we can discover who we really are.

Letting Go of the Personas of Others

"He never pays any attention to me—just plops down on the sofa, grabs the sports section, and I become invisible." Over a cup of coffee, Jane was pouring her heart out, reciting her husband's dismal traits and character flaws, not to mention his imagined intellectual deficiencies. She was lamenting the fact that it's often easier to forgive a criminal his crime than to forgive a husband for hogging the remote. Each day her attitude seemed one of waiting for him to stumble, anticipating the anger and rejection before it could even occur. If he left for a hunting trip (an interest she didn't share) or settled in with beer and basketball on TV (another interest she didn't share), her interior judge sprang into action, and the fight was on.

Her final words to me as we said goodbye were, "Sorry for all the negative spewing this morning—guess I'm just in 'failure mode' today." Jane was in a place familiar to all of us, a discouraging moment when we doubt whether a relationship can be salvaged. We doubt the other person will ever *change*.

Weeks later I encountered her in the grocery store and she came up to me with a spring in her step, smiling broadly. Something had obviously changed. When I asked how things were going, she said simply, "I decided to take responsibility for my own life! I truly have a choice about how I respond to my emotions."

She went on to explain that she had been waiting for her husband to fulfill her list of demands, depending on him to make her happy, employing every manipulative tactic in the book to get him to meet her needs. Finally, she decided to state her feelings clearly and enlist his input into how to make their marriage more mutually satisfying. In the process of those discussions, Jane had a huge "aha" moment. She realized *she must accept him in the same way that she wanted him to accept her.* As she began to schedule activities for herself (without judging him), the two of them were able to focus on the significant issues that *did* unite them in mutually meaningful ways. To her surprise, Jane's husband decided to join her on many more outings of her choosing. As their acceptance of each other as individuals grew, so did their commitment to their unique marriage. And they added yet another significant dimension to their marriage; they approached it as a spiritual discipline, a loving relationship through which they could grow individually and as a couple.

Sometimes we just won't allow people to change. We cling to our judgments of the past. We recite their misdeeds once more. We set their character in concrete. We make projections from our own prejudices. We brand them with indelible labels such as slacker, stupid, sinner, and countless other negative nametags. Conversely, our positive labels—perfect, brilliant, holy, beautiful— can be equally insidious. All labeling places limits on our personhood.

The stories of Jesus, on the other hand, are stories of second chances. The woman at the well was invited to new life as Jesus urged her to let go of the community's stigma as a loose woman (John 4). Nicodemus was astounded by the words of Jesus telling him that he must "be born again from above" (John 3). Throughout the gospels, we find Jesus inviting the lame and the blind to let go of the past and move forward in the newness of God's grace. Can we offer others any less and continue to call ourselves disciples?

Jesus accepted people as they were, where they were. Who among us hasn't thought, "I just want others to accept me as I am"? Surprisingly, we often fail to give to others the acceptance that we demand for ourselves.

In theory, this letting go of our opinions of others may seem easy. In practice, however, we slip into old patterns of "He always does that," "She'll never be any different," "They're just not decent people and never will be." Our limited idea of who people are must be held in the light of God's view of their potential.

While most of the time we cling to negative personas of others, an overly positive view can be damaging as well. We may idealize others in ways that blind us to the truth of their flaws, putting them on such a pedestal that we don't allow them their humanness. Affirming others is one thing; idealizing them is quite another.

Though I still struggle with my rose-colored glasses, now, after one memorable incident, at least I know they are there. Following the conventional wisdom of the 1970s, with its emphasis on preserving self-esteem, I was constantly telling my sons how wonderful they were, how they could do or be anything they desired. One evening David was attending a neighborhood birthday party for one of his middle school buddies. While I thought he was safe and secure a few blocks away, I received a call that four boys had sneaked away from the party to buy beer at a local drive-in. Caught red-handed, they were sent home for parental reprimand. My son was among them, and I was appalled.

During our discussion of the incident, complete with tearful apologies and motherly indignation, David stomped his foot and remarked, "It seems that everything I do disappoints *someone*! Either I make you mad or make my friends mad. I just can't be perfect all the time!"

My insistence that he live up to my expectations and ideals had some unpleasant consequences—for both of us. While in theory it seems reasonable that parental standards help shape the conduct of children, those lofty intentions can easily morph into control and power issues. I soon learned that growing children needed a little wiggle room. The following years contained a number of confrontations, frank discussions, and lots of forgiveness before I finally got it.

The truth is that this Pollyanna way of expecting the best has its shadow side. Often, when I've idealized others, it's made them feel boxed in, constricted by the expectations I projected on them—a kind of psychological hyperbole. Affirmation of good qualities is encouraging. Expecting the best raises the behavioral bar. But we must also give others the freedom to be themselves, to make their own mistakes with the assurance that imperfection is part of the human condition.

It was several years later that I had to come to grips with the difficulty that children have in finding release from parental pressure and unhealthy attachment. I thought I had escaped most of the usual teenage turbulence as David left for college. In fact, I let out a sigh of relief that he was now launched out into the world on his own. On the surface, things had been remarkably smooth, but a storm was building in his psyche that finally erupted in his early twenties. It blindsided me.

The symptoms came on slowly. He began to distance himself emotionally from me, to hide behind a veneer of forced politeness. As a beginning student in medical school, he communicated rarely, but after a while, I couldn't blame it on his demanding schedule. He clearly didn't want to share any of his personal thoughts and struggles with me—a part of our mother-son relationship that had seemed natural and meaningful during his growing-up years.

When I pressed for information or made any attempt to enter the realm of feelings, he retreated to his cave. There were uncharacteristic bursts of anger at the toxic effects of my mothering. He even intimated that something about me had contributed to his father's exit. I was stunned, crushed, deeply hurt; I felt that the last vestiges of my self-esteem had been reduced to rubble. Even if I had failed as a wife, I told myself, I thought I had been an outstanding mother! And now, even that had been called into question.

My woundedness soon turned into anger, of course. One day at an Episcopal retreat conference, I found myself in a spirited conversation with Dr. Robert Moore, the keynote presenter. Before I knew it, I was blurting out my anguish over my relationship with David, cataloguing his sins of neglect and arrogance. By the time I finished my self-righteous little speech, I expected Dr. Moore to validate my feelings and give me permission to confront David with his appalling ingratitude for my dedication as a mother.

I asked, "Don't you think I should tell him exactly how I feel and how much he has hurt me?"

An expert on male psychological development, he surprised me by shrugging his shoulders and saying, "Well, you can do that if you want to." It was apparent he didn't think it was a good idea. Then he added these wise words, "Look, when young men separate from their mothers—and they must—some of them have to cut the apron strings with an ax."

His implication was clear. As a loving parent, I was responsible for letting go of my angst and loving him enough to cut him all the slack he needed. Of course, my deepest desire was for him to develop into a whole human being, separate from me, emotionally healthy and independent. Or did I? Was I clinging to my own need to be needed as a mother? Was I willing to let go of my insistence that he proclaim his "declaration of independence" *my way*?

Sometimes the grace of moments like that brings me to tears. The right person at the right time. The right words at the right time. Once again, I was jolted into awareness of what I was doing and invited to painstaking growth. Buckets of tears and a few days later, I pulled myself together and decided to bite my tongue and wait it out. I had asked Robert Moore one last question, "If I leave him alone, will he ever be back? Will he treat me like he used to?"

"Probably not," he said. "It won't be the same—but I bet he'll come back into relationship with you one of these days."

And he did.

So as we are loosening our grip on our own personas, let's remember to allow those around us to grow and change as well.

Letting Go of God's Persona

God is spirit, and those who worship him must worship in spirit and truth. (John 4:24)

I was sitting on the edge of the bed, listening intently as Sarah told her story. As one of the oldest in the group attending the two-year Academy for Spiritual Formation, I was discovering that I had much to learn from the bright young seminarians in our class. For one week each quarter, our ecumenical class met together to worship, study, share the silence, and open ourselves to a deepening relationship with God in Christ.

Frankly, I had never thought much about inclusive language. My background in the church had been one where the terms Father God, brothers in Christ, and sons of God were used generically. I was accustomed to years of "translation," assuming that even when we sang "Rise Up, O Men of God," that meant me too. I automatically began each prayer with "Heavenly Father," unconsciously imaging the familiar artistic renderings of a pale, white-bearded male.

But I had promised the young women in our class that I would listen openly to their point of view, and I was trying. Sarah explained sadly that it was becoming increasingly difficult for her to relate to roles she couldn't experience; she would never be a "son," a "brother," a "father." As the minister told the congregation, "We must become men of faith," she wondered if he could possibly be talking to her. She felt excluded from the body of Christ, while at the same time knowing full well that her personal encounter with the spirit of Christ was valid and life-changing. I listened and nodded politely, wishing I could relate to the passionate convictions she was expressing.

It was months before her words began to sink in. I remembered the little book written so many years ago by J. B. Phillips, *Your God is Too Small*. I began to meditate on the meaning of John's reminder that "God is Spirit," as well as Paul's words that God was "neither male nor female." And slowly, my narrow view of who and what God is began to expand. In our spiritual journeys in search of God as the "water of life," it seems that we are always coming to the well with a bucket too small. The Spirit spills over the edges of any religious container we use.

An ancient story recorded in Robert Johnson's book, *Owning Your Own Shadow*, describes the process:

The water of life, wishing to make itself known on the face of the earth, bubbled up in a particular place in an artesian well and flowed without effort or limit. People gathered around that well, drank of its life-giving water and were nourished, since it was clean, pure, uncontaminated.

But the people were not content to leave things in this ideal state. Gradually they began to seek to possess the water. They fenced the well and put locks on the gates. They began to put the water in containers and to sell it. They claimed ownership of the well and the property around it. It soon became the property of the powerful and the elite.

The water was greatly offended and angry. It stopped flowing at that place. It left and began bubbling up in another location. Meanwhile, those at the first well were so engrossed in their power systems and the management of the well that they did not notice that the water had vanished. They continued to package and sell the non-existent water and did not notice that the true power was gone.

But some of the dissatisfied, thirsty souls searched with great courage and located the new artesian well. They gathered around it and were once again nourished. Soon, however, that well was under the control of a few and the same fate overtook it. The spring took itself to yet another place, and this has been going on throughout recorded history.[1]

Part of our growth in the Spirit is letting go of the belief that we can ever define God or catch the Spirit in a net of words. After all, a word only points to something beyond itself. The word *sugar* is not sugar itself—one has to taste sugar to actually know its sweetness. We experience God in countless ways, as comforter, as judge, as friend, as peacemaker, as creator, as loving father, as nurturing mother. As human beings, it is often meaningful to us to express God in human terms with human characteristics—that's our major frame of reference. But we need never lose sight of the fact that God is more than the Bible, more than the Church, more than any title, no matter how grandiose, we can devise. When we take one facet of God's nature *and make it the whole*, we tend to distort that which God is: "I am that I am."

Our words will always fall short; our images will always be limited. There is a profound difference between our experience of God and the way we *explain* the experience, between knowing God and talking about God. As writer Karen Armstrong reminds us in *The Spiral Staircase*, "when we are speaking of the reality of God we are at the end of what words or thoughts can usefully do."[2]

As we plod along the spiritual path, we are challenged to let go of our linguistic attempts to define and defend the divine presence. We can't talk our way to God; we can't think our way to God; we can't add and subtract our way to God. Simply put, our words and images of the Holy Mystery are not nearly as important as our *relationship* to it.

As Sarah helped me "reach for a larger container" that day, I felt the anxious transition of letting go of one idea and opening myself to a larger one. I didn't have to let go of the "Heavenly Father" phrase that was so meaningful to me then—I just needed to add to it, to allow the Holy Spirit to expand my horizons. I was to discover during the years ahead that the journey toward the "water of life" was to involve letting go of container after container, until finally there were no words that seemed adequate and no boundaries left.

For Reflection

1. What are your prevalent personas? Which represent the "real" you?

2. Name a mask you wear frequently; what payoff do you get from presenting its characteristics?

3. Think carefully about the automatic assumptions you make about others. What group of people carry specific personas in your mind? Is there some individual that you have pigeonholed? How might you release that judgment?

4. Has your image of God changed through the years? How and why?

Letting Go of Perspectives

The eye is the lamp of the body. So, if your eye is healthy, your whole body
will be full of light; but if your eye is unhealthy, your whole body will be
full of darkness. If then the light in you is darkness, how great is the darkness! (Matt 6:22, RSV)

Your eyes are windows into your body. If you open your eyes wide in wonder and belief, your body fills up with light. If you live squinty-eyed in
greed and distrust, your body is a dank cellar. If you pull the blinds on your
windows, what a dark life you will have! (Matt 6:22)[1]

Sages have always reminded us that it matters how we see things. The biblical
writers spoke of the eye as the lamp of the body. Even contemporary writers
like Haven Kimmel convey a similar message. In his book *The Solace of Leaving
Early*, he writes, "One's perspective is the village one occupies."[2]

Remember the clever fable about the man who fell asleep with limburger
cheese on his mustache? It seems that he woke from a nap, sniffed suspiciously,
and began complaining about the unpleasant odor in his bedroom. He stalked
to the living room, exclaiming, "It smells bad in here, too!" In a huff, he burst
into the open air of the front porch, concluding, "Gee, the whole world stinks!"
He literally took the negative aroma everywhere he went, and his point of view
flavored his world.

We, too, take our perspective with us. We look at life through our own
unique lenses, and that affects everything we see. Rarely do we have the
courage to examine those lenses—those ingrained ways of thinking—to see if
they need to be cleaned up or adjusted. Doing so has a way of challenging our
beliefs, testing our truth, and rattling our theological cages. We usually find
some perspectives that need to be altered or eliminated.

To be sure, this openness to change takes a certain amount of humor and humility. A dear friend and mentor, Dr. Herb Smith, professor emeritus of psychology at Rhodes College in Memphis, often amused students with a tattered note he kept tucked in his shirt pocket and boldly wore to class. With a twinkle in his eye, he would read it to us: "What I'm saying today reflects my current understanding and is not to be confused with the ultimate truth." He embodied this rare willingness to change his mind if and when clearer revelation presented itself.

If we consider altering our understanding of something, it doesn't necessarily mean that last week we were wrong and today we are right. If we're sincerely open to growth, God continues to deepen and expand our understanding of life in the dynamic movement of the Holy Spirit. Most of us are not comfortable with that level of openness, and our anxiety level soars. What if we don't *get it right*? As a wise person once told me, "Perhaps the faith journey is not meant to turn our anxiety into answers, but rather to turn our anxiety into *awe*."

An important layer of the letting-go process involves a close examination of the perspectives that filter our view of the world at large and our lives in particular. Our unspoken need to have things black and white, cut and dried, right or wrong, perfect or flawed, can serve as chains that constrict our freedom and growth. What perspectives might you need to let go so that you can see life as the miraculous adventure that it is?

"I Must Get It Right"

> Most of the crimes in this world have been committed by people who thought they were right. —Richard Rohr[3]

Being right is highly over-rated. Even our cherished dream of being able to say, "I told you so," never feels quite as good as we think it will. And "sweet revenge" is not really sweet at all; it leaves a rancid aftertaste in the depths of the soul. Even Jesus didn't appear to place much stock in right answers. The gospel accounts mention 183 questions asked of him, and he answers only three!

Many of us would rather be right than happy. The reality is, however, that the compulsion to be right can thwart and limit our communication with others. We've all experienced conversations that deteriorated into a ping-pong game of one-up-man-ship. We know what it's like to give an opinion, only to realize that the other person is busy formulating a rebuttal rather than a response. We also know the feeling of intense competition that wells up inside us as we get attached to winning the verbal battle—the stuff of which ulcers are made and friends are lost.

In addition, the determination to be right—to win—prevents us from learning the crucial difference between tolerance and acceptance. We pat ourselves on the back when we reach a point of tolerance for the opinions of others. We will be magnanimous enough to "allow" them to have opinions contrary to ours. We might even go so far as to agree not to interfere with their practice or beliefs, to refrain from trying to convince them of the rightness of our position. However, this level of tolerance still carries an unspoken tinge of judgment, a silent message that "I'm right and you're wrong."

Acceptance goes a step farther. It implies a willingness to consider that others' points of view are as valid for them as yours is for you. It admits the possibility that you might not have all the answers, that you might not see the whole picture.

There is a pithy prayer from Kenya that conveys this message:

From the cowardice that dares not face new truth,
From the laziness that is contented with half-truth,
From the arrogance that thinks it knows all truth,
Good Lord, deliver me.[4]

In the late 1980s I was enrolled in some lay courses at Perkins School of Theology at Southern Methodist University in Dallas. In those days, there was very little cross-cultural learning between eastern and western traditions. A tacit division existed between believers and pagans, us and them. I found myself in a class on some aspect of Christian orthodoxy, taught by a Jesuit priest who had been reared in Japan by missionary parents. He was the first Christian I had ever met who embodied a guilt-free blend of east and west.

Some of us in the class were drawn to his easy embrace of both the Buddhist and Christian traditions, and we stayed after class to bombard him with questions. He told us how the meditation practices of Buddhism had enhanced his prayer life and facilitated the deepening of his Christian faith. Smiling, he pointed upward and said, "We are fingers pointing to the Moon. We gaze longingly on the mystery called God, and we try to show each other the way. Let's not argue about the fingers; instead let's continue to point to the Moon." Something inside me relaxed and expanded. Maybe I could begin to be honest about my affinity for eastern meditation techniques, my inner conviction that they had something sacred to teach me.

I began to let go of my arrogant perspective that Christianity had a corner on the truth. I could finally allow the all-inclusive love of God to be a mystery—I didn't have to have it totally figured out, nor did I have to suppress my natural inclination toward the words of truth coming from other sources. Jesus was God incarnate for me; Christian symbols and stories continue to shape and form my faith journey, but at last I realized that *Christianity is my standing place, not my horizon.*

Unfortunately, many of us have a deep-down conviction that we must get it right for God. I remember an example of the sadness and poignancy of this mindset. A friend whose young husband was terminally ill was a devoted Christian and stalwart believer in the power of prayer. Though she, along with every prayer group in the city, was praying for his healing, the condition continued to worsen. As we were talking one day, my heart broke to hear her say,

"John just keeps getting worse, Linda. I don't know what I'm doing wrong—I guess I'm not praying right."

What a sad statement about our view of God! It says in effect that we believe God is sitting out there somewhere withholding healing until we spout the proper formula. Who would want to worship such a God? Scripture tells us that God hears the prayers of our hearts, not our lofty, well-formed phrases. Better still, we are assured that the "Spirit intercedes with sighs too deep for words" (Rom 8:26b). Our yearnings engage the spirit on our behalf. We pray and trust the mysterious outcome to a loving God.

Our need to get it right also makes it difficult to utter words that are crucial to our soul's honesty: "I just don't know." One Easter Sunday I was having a particularly troublesome time with some of the scriptural resurrection language—the conflict between biblical accounts, the resulting questions about bodily resurrection that are familiar to any thinking Christian. I considered the many translations that had occurred between the original Greek and the English version on my bookshelf. What was the *right* interpretation? Actual or metaphorical? Physical body or spiritual body? As I sat in the choir loft, fumbling through the hymnal for the closing hymn, I was disturbed by my own doubts and questions.

With the anxiety still swirling, I stood as the organ began a tune so well-known to me that I closed the hymnbook. It was "In the Garden," a surprising choice, I thought, for Easter Sunday. As I sang the simple words of the old gospel hymn from memory, my eyes fell on the magnificent stained glass window in the rear of the church, depicting Jesus in a garden. The familiar words of the song stood out with fresh clarity, "And he walks with me, and he talks with me, and he tells me I am his own." An inner voice whispered, "Just experience that . . . just know that. It's enough; don't sweat the details." Then I felt a poke in the ribs, as the alto next to me handed me a tissue. . . . my face was wet with tears of relief. I didn't have to get it right after all.

"I Must Be Sure"

Underneath our desire to be right is a desperation to be absolutely sure about everything. Someone told me once that one of the greatest enemies of spiritual growth is *certainty*. Being too sure about too many things makes us rigid and unteachable. That seemed a bit radical to me until I had a revealing dream one night at a critical time in my journey.

I was walking steadily up a narrow path, just wide enough for one person, with a ditch on either side. As I climbed, people would occasionally appear down in the ditches on either side, waving me on with encouraging smiles. I was anticipating something rewarding if I could just reach the top. Finally I arrived at a precipice, and as I stood there, there was nothing in front of me but black emptiness—no stars, no moon, no net to catch me, nothing. There was a strong need to jump into the abyss with no assurance, with nothing but the belief, the hope, that something would catch me, but my heart was pounding with anxiety. I jumped.

As I recalled that dream through the following weeks and months, yearning to be shown its significance, some insights began to surface. The dream seemed to be inviting me to *experience* God, rather than continue to learn about God and to abandon the predictable path that I could *see*. I had always relished the intellectual spiritual quest—gobbling up new books, seeking gifted teachers, enrolling in yet another Bible course. In all honesty, I was more likely to read ten books on prayer than to pray! Through the dream, I was being asked to let go of my previous assumptions about who and what God was and embark instead on a visceral relationship that was different from being able to recite the appropriate Bible verse. But first, I had to befriend the unknown, to let go of certainty, to learn the meaning of trust.

Unfortunately, this means *not knowing what will happen*. We read with eager acceptance the promises of Jesus that we shall "have life abundant." We'll take it, thank you very much! However, the reality is that we want to be certain that it is *our* definition of abundance, thereby continuing to maintain control rather than relinquish it.

We're like the man who answered the preacher's altar call, marched down to the front of the church, fell to his knees, and said, "O God, I'm giving my life to you. And to show my sincerity, I've made a long list of all that I'm going to accomplish for you." Immediately, a booming voice answers, "Is that all?" The embarrassed man returns to his pew, gets out his pencil, and expands his list. He returns to the altar and implores God again, "O God, I've added more to our contract." Again God replies, "Is that all?" A third time, the man returns with his list of intentions, and finally God says in exasperation, "Look, just sign it, and let *me* fill it in!"

Most of us derive a sense of security from the *illusion* that we know what the future will be. Letting go of this illusion leaves a hollowed-out space through which the Spirit can blow fresh air. This is not a passive posture where we sit in a "spiritual recliner" and wait for God to act. It is a participating posture where we wait and watch in prayerful anticipation, ready to act in concert with divine guidance.

God's guidance usually evolves one step at a time. Rather than wait for the entire agenda to be laid before us, we're called simply to take the next step, moving to the point of light that we can see at that time, without attempting to control the outcome. We launch out in trust. Have you ever noticed how glibly we use the word *trust*? If we insist on knowing what will happen, then why is *faith* necessary? The concepts of trust and faith both involve the willingness to risk.

Like many aspects of letting go, the desire for certainty keeps returning, wearing another set of clothes. As I was wrestling with the decision about whether to accept the opportunity to write this book, I found myself once again confronting a familiar demon. Questions were engulfing me: Are you sure you're not too old to embark on a project like this? Aren't you ready to kick back and enjoy your adorable grandchildren? Aren't you afraid of what people will think? How will you find the time? And above all: How can you be sure you won't *fail*?

One day, as I sat with a spiritual direction client who was in the midst of a discernment issue, I heard myself saying to her, "Faith always involves taking a risk. There's an element of the unknown—that's where trust comes in."

As my client left the office, I felt like a fraud. I was clearly not practicing what I was preaching. God seemed to be speaking to me through the sound of my own words, and I knew I had to leave certainty behind me once again.

It is said that one of the major challenges of spiritual growth is the increasing capacity to tolerate ambivalence and paradox. To that I would add *uncertainty*.

"I Must Be Perfect"

The fruit of perfectionism comes in a mixture of flavors. It begins with the sweet taste of excellence; after all, our culture encourages us to "aim high." However, the sour aftermath of perfectionism can undermine and infect the whole tree.

In her landmark book, *When the Heart Waits*, Sue Monk Kidd deals with this perspective as she describes "The Tinsel Star":

> The Tinsel Star pours herself into a long line of praiseworthy accomplishments. She's the overachiever in us, the perfectionist, the performer whose outer radiance often covers an inner insecurity. Whether it's being mom, career woman, church volunteer, or committee chair, the Tinsel Star's aim is to do it with dazzle and win accolades. When we adopt this particular ego mask, we invest ourselves in the notion that those who shine the brightest are loved the most.[5]

Perfectionists grow up worshipping false ideals that proclaim in chorus:

- Do it better and you'll be noticed.

- Be noticed and you'll be applauded.

- Be applauded and you'll be the best.

- Be the best and you'll be *loved*.

Our culture joins in with precepts such as "Never ever give up!" "Second place is for losers!" "Nothing but the best!" Of course, those who answer the call to perfectionism are rewarded with applause and admiration, so the effort to excel is redoubled.

That's the good news. The bad news is that perfectionism can separate you from others and starve your soul. And it can take a tragic toll on your relationships. If you're always trying to do it perfectly, you lack the courage and clarity to face your own faults. The possibility of failure becomes intolerable, so you are reluctant to take risks; that idealistic persona (your false self) has to be maintained at all costs. You end up attempting only those things you're certain you can do well. You cease to stretch your horizons, to live past the edge of your abilities, to *grow*. You start sugar-coating your problems and polishing your performance.

Inadvertently, perfectionism creates an unwelcoming atmosphere for others—one in which they don't feel free to be honest about their own shortcomings. It's difficult to expose your own failures and frustrations to someone who appears to have none of his own. In some strange and beautiful way, our shared *im*perfections unite us in a bond of common humanity.

When word came to me—more than once—that some of my departing husband's discontent was a response to my perfectionism, I was defensive. After all, I had been doggedly devoted to the good-wife syndrome, producing well-balanced meals (*always* on time) and an orderly house, along with being an entertaining hostess and supportive partner—always striving to be someone a husband could be proud of. In trying to become supremely efficient, I forgot to be *real*. In trying to create an idyllic environment, I inadvertently created an atmosphere where anger, conflict, and misbehavior were considered unacceptable. The storybook setting provided an ideal foil for everyone's shadow stuff. In order to fit into this conflict-free atmosphere, family members stuffed anything negative down an emotional rabbithole.

Therein lies the resulting paradox. Perfectionists usually end up being admired rather than cherished, appreciated rather than loved. They are envied for their accomplishments, yet distanced because of them. The love they hope to engender dies on the vine, or they somehow distance the ones they love and attract those who love them only conditionally. In any event, they don't get the love they so desperately want. So the perfectionist just tries harder—a vicious cycle.

Many of us have had to learn the hard way that it's an imperfect world and that we are its flawed inhabitants. When my husband asked for a divorce, my illusion of perfection was shattered for all the world to see. I had to face my imperfect self who, no matter how I tried, couldn't save this broken marriage. Unrealistic expectations and unexplored mid-life dysfunction on both our parts continued to muddy the waters. Regardless of the other factors involved in the break-up, I was forced to begin the painstaking process of letting go of perfectionism in all its pretty disguises.

Understandably, perfectionists are chronically discontented—when you're a perfectionist, nothing seems to measure up to the projected ideal, not even yourself. Your husband should be more attentive, your co-workers should be more appreciative, your children should study harder, your waistline should be smaller. It's an unending cycle of unfulfilled expectations.

Here are a few behavioral hints that signal perfectionist tendencies:

● You wake up at three in the morning obsessing over the one criticism you received about your speech, amid a host of accolades.

- You put off giving the dinner party until you've painted the living room, repaved the driveway, and perfected the recipe for crème brûlée.

- You overlook the satisfaction of *doing* something, because your focus is on getting it finished with success.

- You live with an invisible judge inside you who constantly critiques your performance.

Basically, we perfectionists need to learn self-acceptance and let the air out of our overblown expectations. We will be met with some surprising rewards—foremost, the freedom to be ourselves. And that authenticity frees others to be themselves in our company, making us more approachable, more safe, more *real*. After all, to be spiritually authentic is not to hide behind a phony mask that never shows pain or a façade that never cracks.

This integrated wholeness is actually what the scriptures seem to suggest when the word "perfection" is used. In Marjorie Thompson's *The Way of Forgiveness*, she writes:

> When Jesus calls us to "be perfect, therefore, as your heavenly Father is perfect" (Matt 5:48), he clearly does not mean a pinched, legalistic concept of perfection—the very thing he has been warning against in each instance! He points rather to a deep, God-designed wholeness in the human spirit. We cannot make ourselves perfect by our own efforts. Wholeness is a gift that comes to us gradually through the process of daily living with God.[6]

Many wisdom traditions across the world seem to reflect this same integration of flaws, even incorporating the idea into their cultural habits. In *My Grandfather's Blessings*, Rachel Naomi Remen tells us that Zen gardeners leave one fat dandelion in the midst of the precise patterns of a formal mediation garden. In the weaving of exquisite rugs in Iran, skilled rug weavers intentionally include an error called "The Persian Flaw." Even in Puritan America, the finest quilters deliberately left a drop of their own blood on every quilt they made, while Native Americans wove a broken bead, the "spirit bead," into every beaded creation. Writes Remen: "When life weaves a spirit bead into your very fabric, you may stumble upon a wholeness greater than you had dreamed possible before."[7]

"I Must Be Liked"

I have a friend whose motto is: "What other people think of me is none of my business." A lofty ideal, cleverly stated, but the truth is that most of us want the approval of others. In fact, we want that approval so desperately that it's easy to fall into the trap of deciding what we *think* others *think* about us. Then we suppose what they want and expect from us. It's a deadly spiral of projection that leads away from the authentic self we yearn for.

In *The Clear and Simple Way* author Judith Ann Parsons puts it in plain language: "It is better to be disliked for who you are than to be liked for who you are not—the only thing you really have to share with any one, anyway, is your own state of being."[8]

As we summon the courage to let go of our tendencies to be pleasers and perfectionists, it doesn't take long to discover that the driving force behind such behavior is an insatiable need for approval. We deplete our centeredness by giving away our power in tiny bits and pieces. Before we know it, we have adapted to this or agreed to that and have placed our sense of worth in the hands of others. We find ourselves in the precarious place of allowing others to tell us who we are and *believing* it. It makes chameleons of us.

At what point does flexibility become adaptation? And when does that adaptation become toxic to the soul? The pivotal point varies with each person, and no one can define it for us. For me, it's a matter of sensing that fine line where the cost is too high, when I'm not being true to myself. Then it becomes my responsibility to cry, "Enough!" Unfortunately many of us habitually say "yes" when our silent souls are saying "no." It's up to us to set boundaries to safeguard our health and well-being. We can learn that "no" is a complete sentence and need not be followed by our excuses, manufactured or real.

The development of this harmful perspective starts early. As a youngster, an unusual need for approval seemed to be a part of who I was. I remember a constant compulsion to be the best speller, to know the right answer, to wear the appropriate dress, to have the proper belief, to make a good impression—all in an unconscious effort to gain the esteem of others. The very thought of disappointing someone filled me with a deep sense of anguish and unworthiness.

My undefined sense of self was especially fragile in my marriage, as I repeatedly sought to shape my behavior into conventional compliance. My husband became involved in judging beauty pageants, and my soul tried to scream. I was convinced that it was my duty to accompany him on the occasional week-long jaunts around the country, and I lacked the courage and clarity to say I didn't want to go. Leaving our young sons for such a frivolous pursuit seemed like a poor choice to me, but as usual, I shushed my inner opposition and continued to pursue what I believed to be the proper course of conduct—submit and smile, smile and submit. After all, I had been taught that a good wife and mother puts the needs of her husband and children first—in that order. I wasn't willing to give my family a single opening for criticism, if I could possibly help it. I was dependent on their approval to make me feel worthwhile.

This need can spread its tentacles into every part of our lives, and most of the time, we don't realize how it subconsciously drives our actions. In fact, perhaps the most serious barrier to being *real* is the psychic presence of the question: *how am I coming across?* We then see the world through an egocentric lens that leads straight to self-deception, and eventually to distortion and manipulation.

It reveals itself in insidious ways that seem okay to us because they are such familiar mental companions:

Do I look okay?
Did I say something wrong?
I don't think they like me.
I'm sure she thinks I'm silly, but . . .
He's avoiding me.
They gave me the cold shoulder.

Or, conversely, our ego can eagerly grab flattery or fortune to affirm us:

They complimented my speech, so that must mean it was okay.
I got invited to that party, so I'm important.
She saved me a seat, so that means she approves of me.
I made a bundle on that deal, so God is rewarding me.
I've read all those books, so I'm smarter than the others.

This natural, but damaging, ego investment in the approval of others rarely leaves permanently. It surprises us with sneak attacks. Christine thought she had that particular neediness under control, until one day when she read to a discussion group a poem she had recently written. One person was so moved that she requested a copy of it. However, the leader of the group said something dismissive, and Christine's inner wound was ripped open.

"Five years ago, I would have stopped writing," Christine admitted. "I would have been devastated by that person's rejection. But this time, it was different. I could *see* what was happening. It hurt, that's for sure. But soon I became conscious of my wounded reaction, acknowledged it, and said, 'Thanks for sharing, but you're no longer in charge!'" Christine saw the truth that others could disappoint her, disapprove of her, or reject her, but they couldn't tell her *who she was*. She would no longer allow the opinions of others to define her worth.

When our energy is directed toward the protection of our fragile egos, we constrict our freedom to be true to ourselves and love our neighbors with sacred abandon. Letting go of the need for approval means that we can become independent of the good and bad opinions of others. But first, we must become aware of the myriad ways we embody this behavior, making us harmfully vulnerable to both criticism and flattery. For me, at least, it has turned into a lifetime project.

"I Must Stay Young"

When I ran into Monica in the department store, I barely recognized her. We had been casual friends twenty or thirty years ago, and it was a pleasure to catch up on the intervening years. However, I couldn't help noticing her unlined face, her taut skin, her somewhat myopic look. To tell the truth, her face didn't match her hands—or her veins, or her slightly thickening waistline, or her years. Our personal history told me that we were both in our sixties. Where were *her* crow's feet?

I found myself envying her youthful look, yet being somewhat judgmental about the expensive procedure that was responsible for it. But I had no right to my smugness. Didn't I, too, lament the ravages of age and try to do everything imaginable not to look old? Somewhere in my soul, I knew there was an unspoken difference between good personal care and frantically clutching the image of the younger self. It wasn't a time for judgment; it was a time to examine my own motives. And, granted, scores of lives have been drastically improved by the miracles of reconstructive procedures. Somehow, however, we must find a way to measure ourselves differently, to see ourselves as more than a body and a brain. As a dear friend said as she was dealing with the effects of chemotherapy, "I am *more* than my hair!"

As author Ram Dass dealt with the aftermath of a debilitating stroke, he shared some of the wisdom he received in *Still Here: Embracing Aging, Changing, and Dying*:

> [Our efforts to look young] remind me of someone rushing around the fields in the autumn painting the marvelous gold and red leaves with green paint. Lots of time and energy wasted. . . . The images our culture generates are designed to make you feel that aging is a kind of failure; that somehow God made a big mistake. If God were as smart as the commercials, people would be young forever, but since God isn't, only the wonders of science and commerce can save us. How bizarre.[9]

Our obsession with youth is not always about appearance, of course. Many seek out younger marriage partners, take on physical challenges usually associated with the young, retain childish behaviors, or start running with a younger crowd. Others seem unable to move beyond their yearning to relive the high school ball games, the college pranks, or their children's successes and failures. No matter what picture of the past we cling to, we seem intent on slowing down the clock.

This negative attitude toward aging permeates not only our own behavior, but also the attitudes of others *toward us* in ways that are difficult to discern. I must admit that lately I've begun to notice tiny signs of ageism directed at me, signs that are so subtle that it took me awhile to acknowledge it to myself. Younger people tend to talk *around* mature folks like me instead of *to* us, as if they were simply being courteous. I notice their eyes leaving mine during the conversation, traveling over my shoulder to survey the room to see who else might be more interesting. There is no malice involved, because mostly no one is conscious of it. It hurts, though.

These experiences remind me of times when care-givers would come to my father's nursing home room, addressing their questions to me—the daughter and visitor—rather than to him, even though he was perfectly capable of answering himself. Now that I'm getting older, I'm becoming aware of how much that must have hurt and diminished him.

I sometimes read with wistfulness the accounts of ancient societies that revered their elders, that valued the accumulated wisdom of years spent in the trenches of life. Our media bombard us with the icons of youthful beauty with such persistence that our greatest compliments for the elderly are, "She doesn't look sixty-five, does she?" or "It's amazing how well he's holding up!" However, lest we blame the faceless media again, let's admit the myriad ways that we believe the propaganda and participate in the problem.

Millions are spent (by both men and women) on creams and cures, procedures and promises in an attempt to halt the aging process—or at least to hide it. We voluntarily support popular TV shows featuring radical makeovers and drastic surgeries, while very little applause is given for late-life wisdom and the inherent beauty of soul shining through.

There's a tricky balance here, I know. I'm as gullible as the next aging consumer when a new miracle potion hits the market. But shouldn't we at least examine the futility of grasping something that we're destined to lose? A piercing look at our complicity in this false ideal of eternal youth will reveal that we have a tough time letting go of the younger self.

"Life Is Just One Struggle After Another"

It had become a familiar refrain. Every time we met for lunch, Clara would plop down breathlessly in the chair, full of excuses for being her usual fifteen minutes late.

So much to be done, so little time.

So much pressure, so little relief.

So many demands, so little energy.

Soon, though, *very soon*, things would surely settle down. They never have.

This mindset can sabotage our serenity like a wet, gray cloud. We begin to see life as a series of obstacles to be hurdled, rather than moments to be relished. And, of course, as soon as we solve the current crisis, *then* "everything will be okay." In other words, we spend our days preparing to live, rather than living.

If we're not waiting for things to cool down, then sometimes we're waiting for them to heat up! Roger has been searching for a "meaningful relationship" for as long as I can remember. "If I could only meet the right woman," he dreams, investing all his happiness in another person and leaving his own quest for wholeness untended and unappreciated.

This perspective often expands to a sort of cosmic cynicism, a conviction that "the world is going to hell in a hand-basket." If you counter this pessimistic view, you may be dubbed "out of touch with reality." Not necessarily so. One can choose to follow the example of Jesus, who

- recognized evil, but chose not to live in it.

- recognized danger, but chose not to dwell in fear.

- recognized hate, but chose love.

Yes, we learn from the lessons of life. Yes, life presents compelling challenges. But this persistent perspective of constant struggle can create a lens through which the life we *experience* becomes a series of somber days to slog through. Letting it go can open the way to joy and sunshine.

"We're the Best!"

> For by the grace given to me I say to everyone among you not to think of yourself more highly than you ought to think, but to think with sober judgment... (Rom 12:3)

This is another perspective that appears positive on the surface, but whose shadow can overtake us. Few of us would admit to a feeling of superiority, but we delude ourselves. Sometimes this attitude of inflation can be masked behind a cloak of false humility or patronizing helpfulness. However, if we look closely, we can see that our actions and attitudes betray us.

For instance, in the glow of the patriotism that strengthens us as a country, we are often caught up in divisive and damaging perspectives that undermine our spiritual growth as people and as a nation in insidious ways. We want to affirm the best about America, but sometimes we do that by diminishing others. Much of our religious language—and certainly our political discourse—stands in stark contrast to the humility and generosity promoted not only in the Bible, but also in other sacred texts. In following the premise that "Might makes right," we have, unwittingly perhaps, confused fear with respect. We often *act* out of a love of power and *call* it the power of love.

We can see subtle signs in the words we use, the jokes we make, the dismissive looks. Every time we make a snide remark about another, every time we condescend, every time we make sweeping judgments about classes or races or nationalities—every time we categorize into "them" and "us," we distance ourselves from the loving, inclusive spirit of Christ and from our highest selves.

Writes Erik Kolbell in *What Jesus Meant: The Beatitudes and a Meaningful Life*:

> We've so institutionalized competition that it's become a bedrock of who we are. We put enormous pressure on ourselves to be triumphant at the expense of being caring. . . . We make it too costly to commit errors, admit mistakes, fall short, not know the answer, ask for a second chance, ask for directions, or ask for forgiveness, let alone hope that forgiveness will be granted.[10]

Of course, Kolbell recognizes the dilemma this presents. Uh-oh, does this mean "mercy reduces us to the disposition of a lamb without the muscle of a lion?" He clearly believes it is possible to stand for justice, hold people accountable for the consequences of their actions, and still show the same mercy that God shows us. Mercy and justice are not mutually exclusive.

The divided perspective of us-and-them weakens rather than strengthens us individually and collectively, overshadowing the sense of common humanity Jesus encouraged with spiritual pride and haughty self-righteousness. For when we possess an inflated sense of our own goodness, watch out. Our own power to judge and punish another's misdeeds soon outweighs our need to confess our own. Can we let go of this hubris and choose some humility instead?

Kolbell uses eloquent words as he envisions the church's mission: To create a world where ". . . the dignity of work is affirmed by a decent paycheck, where colors that distinguish us don't divide us, where the pride of patriotism doesn't dissolve into the arrogance of nationalism, and where nature's beauty is revered rather than ravaged."[11]

"I Must Believe That"

"I'm just not willing to check my brain at the church door," he said. "Does the church require that I sacrifice my intellectual integrity?" Richard was expressing the frustration felt by many genuine seekers of God who want a safe and accepting environment in which to explore their spiritual yearning, even if it includes doubt. They agree with the clever analogy that likens the mind to a parachute. It functions only when open.

In the practice of spiritual direction (guidance is a more appropriate term), I encounter people along all points of the faith continuum—those who are devout church-going disciplinarians and those who are, for one reason or another, alienated from the church. And I have found that simply going to church doesn't necessarily make you a Christian any more than going to a garage makes you a mechanic. Since part of my task as spiritual guide is to help folks listen deeply to the voice of God in their everyday experience, I am privileged to witness the nature of honest spiritual struggle. And I'm convinced that God does not frown upon authentic doubt. After all, it can be the cutting edge of faith.

The truth is that some churches welcome a searching spirit of questioning and some don't. Some churches perpetuate the idea that merely repeating a series of words buys you a ticket to heaven, and those magic words are defined by the church. However, mastering the rules, so to speak, is often a far cry from the process of developing a compassionate heart. Nowhere in Scripture does Jesus give a more graphic illustration of heart knowledge versus head knowledge than in his parable of the sheep and the goats, recorded in Matt 25:

> Come, you that are blessed by my Father, inherit the kingdom prepared for you from the foundation of the world; for I was hungry and you gave me food, I was thirsty and you gave me something to drink, I was a stranger and you welcomed me, I was naked and you gave me clothing, I was sick and you took care of me, I was in prison and you visited me . . . just as you did it to one of the least of these who are members of my family, you did it to me.

So beliefs, though they may be comforting, have little transformative value in and of themselves. We box ourselves in with doctrine and dogma, some that expand our spirits and some that contract our spirits. Only by testing in the arena of experience can we infuse our creeds with a beating heart. Beliefs must be lived and breathed, not merely spoken.

In simple terms, the Greek root for *to believe* means *to give one's heart to*. This may or may not involve any particular head knowledge. After all, the people addressed in the parable did not even *know* they had been ministering "to Jesus." Their response reveals their bewilderment: "Lord, when was it that we saw you hungry, thirsty . . . a stranger, or naked?" (Matt 25:37–39).

They acted from the heart, rather than the head. Their compassionate deeds grew out of who they *were* and were obviously based on a relationship with God rather than a creed. An inspiring theology professor, Dr. Glenn Hinson, reminded me one day with a knowing smile, "God is not as fastidious as we are about theology and religious methods."

Unfortunately, many of our beliefs may keep us from deepening this relationship. Through the past few years of sharing the struggles and stories of others, I've noticed that certain perspectives keep showing up as blinking red lights that retard growth. What follows is a random and incomplete list, but perhaps it will spur you to cast a discerning eye on beliefs that might be limiting your journey.

"It's God's Will"

Sometimes the question "why?" gives us spiritual paralysis. Of course, it's the natural response of any caring person when confronted with the tragedies of life that seem so grossly unfair and unspeakable. However, in our compulsion to know the answers to life's hard questions, we make some pretty rash assumptions. In our quest to find the cause and thereby place the blame, when all else fails, some of us malign the character of God by making God responsible for everything—God's in control, so God did it. We accuse God of things that would seem criminal acts in human beings.

My favorite analogy for God's role in life's tragedies was passed along by author Flora Wuellner when she was teaching us at the Academy for Spiritual Formation.

She said something like this: "It's one thing to say that if my child falls down the concrete stairs and breaks his leg, I as a good parent will do everything in my power to bring something good out of that experience—I'll read to him, teach him that he shouldn't have left his rollerblades at the top of the stairs, help him heal, love him through the experience of pain and recovery. However, it's quite another thing to say that as a good parent, I would *push* that child down the stairs *in order that* he can learn those valuable lessons!"

I'm not willing to believe that God engineers the pain in our lives to foster our growth, but I *am* willing to affirm the words of Rom 8:28, "All things work together for good for those who love God." The hope for healing and growth is found in our willing participation in the spiritual dynamic implied by that powerful verse of Scripture. No matter how the circumstances came about, God invites us to be involved in our own healing process, working with God to pick up the broken pieces and fashion them into something new. Our finite minds can never know in this life the mysterious reasons why things happen as they do. There finally comes a point at which we can let go of those questions of causation and concentrate on our faithful response. It is better to accept the mystery than to define it incorrectly.

"The Bible Is Literally True"

It isn't the point of this book to debate the issue of biblical inerrancy. However, as I watch people wrestle with each printed word (as if the biblical writers had actually written in English!), it saddens me when the Bible is used as a weapon with which to frighten folks into submission rather than a liberating revelation of truth. There is a danger of becoming so embroiled in the words that one forgets to commune with the Living Word. The Bible is not a God to be worshipped; it is a written revelation designed to lead us to the experience of God. Nor do I believe the Bible is the *only* revelation of God. "Earth's crammed with heaven," wrote Elizabeth Barrett Browning, and evidences of God lurk right under our busy, distracted little noses. There are enough examples to fill a library, for the world is infused with the holy.

I experience God when my grandchild says, "I love you, Lindy."

I experience God when I sit on a piece of driftwood at sunrise on the beach and watch that red ball of fire peek over the horizon.

I experience God when I see heroic responses to those in need.

I experience God in the beautiful burst of love between two people.

I experience God when I hear the thunder of a grand organ as it booms out Bach's "Toccata and Fugue in D Minor."

I also experience God in the words of Isa 40:31, the Bible verse closest to my heart: "Those who wait upon the Lord shall renew their strength, they shall mount up with wings like eagles, they shall run and not be weary; they shall walk and not faint."

Obviously, the Bible is a chronicle of salvation history—stories of people expressing their experience of God *as they saw it, given their cultural and historical context.* It is not meant to be used as a chronological history of events. In the matter of literal interpretation of Scripture, Rabbi Micah Greenstein of Temple Israel in Memphis issued a humorous, but pointed, challenge from the guest pulpit at Calvary Episcopal Church. He urged everyone to read Deut 21, which calls for the execution of children who are rebellious and disobedient to their parents. He then remarked, "If that commandment were taken literally, none of us would survive!"

I rest my case.

"Self-Care is Selfish"

My anxiety level was through the roof. Filling my days with frantic busyness, micro-managing my young sons' lives, and fretting over their adjustment to my divorce were taxing the limits of my sanity. And then I heard some simple words that shifted my gears: "Linda, the best gift you can give your children is a *sane* mother!"

The words bounced against a perspective that was firmly entrenched in my psyche, for I had long equated self-care with selfishness and ego-centeredness. I was about to learn the difference. As I pursued the path of "dedication till you drop," it became increasingly difficult to give out of an empty cup. My well of spiritual, physical, and emotional energy was approaching bone-dry, and soon there would be nothing left of me to give anyone.

So what would enhance my sanity, I wondered? Since I wasn't accustomed to the question, the answers didn't come at first. Then I began to notice intentionally some little things that nurtured me—a fragrant soak in the tub with a candle burning, settling against a pile of pillows with a compelling novel, quiet walking prayers, chopping fresh vegetables and cooking a huge pot of soup to share. And I also became aware that the company of some people lifted my spirits and others lifted my despair. Some of those closest to my heart were kept at arm's length for a while, because their righteous anger on my behalf eventually became toxic to my healing, even though at first it made me feel supported. In short, I had to take responsibility for my own sanity by seizing every nurturing moment I possibly could.

Sometimes an emotional wound has to be bandaged and tended carefully as God's natural healing process takes over. We must find ways to support our own sanity and let go of the notion that such self-nurture is selfish. In fact, I finally realized that tending to my own well-being was the only way I could ever enhance the lives of others.

"Solitude Is Slothful"

I used to think silent prayer was little more than a waste of time that could and *should* be more productive. Why sit quietly when one could be really *doing* something? Besides, what if I "listened to God" and didn't hear anything?

The practice of silence had to change my life before I could change my mind. My immature assumption that silent prayer was simply a matter of closing one's mouth and allowing the mind to continue chattering underwent a radical change in my midlife years. I stumbled upon *The Cloud of Unknowing*, a thirteenth-century contemplative text, and I was intrigued by its mystical message about the nature of prayer, about the value of getting beyond and behind our spoken words. I knew that the text from John 4:24, stating that "God is Spirit, and those who worship God must worship in spirit" obviously pointed to some sort of wordless communication. I knew I didn't have the tools or the experience in prayer to fully comprehend the book, but its message just wouldn't leave me alone. I was destined to deal with the silence.

Fortunately, someone gave me a metaphor that finally clicked: Silent prayer is not the silence of a graveyard, but the silence of a garden growing. If you stand in the midst of a winter garden, it appears that absolutely nothing is happening in the deadening stillness. Yet even our memories of elementary biology remind us that there is vigorous activity, cellular movement, unseen life underneath the ground that will eventually emerge in leaves and flowers and, ultimately, fruit. Suddenly I knew that same process would work for my soul's growth, if I could just learn how to be still.

Something in me responded to the challenge, but my extroverted self wanted companions, someone to explore the silence *with*. Once again, I couldn't find any.

In retrospect, I'm grateful that a higher wisdom prevailed. So great was my dependence on sharing the journey with others that I doubt I'd have done the inner work necessary to befriend the silence if I could have found someone to *talk* with about it. My companion appeared in the form of a book by Father Thomas Keating, giving me step-by-step instructions in the centering prayer method, which he described as a path to contemplative prayer. I decided to trust Keating's guidance.

As I read his book, *Open Mind, Open Heart,*[12] I dutifully followed his rules, rising early each morning to sit in silence, trusting that God was tilling the soil of my soul in ways that I could not control nor measure. For a person so accustomed to being proactive, to managing my spiritual quest through planning, learning, and *trying harder*, it was the toughest discipline I ever undertook. At first, the silence seemed to be my enemy, as a cacophony of chattering voices competed for attention, but I continued to doggedly follow Keating's instructions to "return to the sacred word." I'll admit that many times, my feelings ranged from "This is ridiculous" to "I really need to empty the dishwasher instead of sitting here." But I had been reading the works of other contemporary leaders in spiritual formation telling me that the very language of God is silence. If I were ever going to learn to hear the voice of God, I knew I had to present my soul as an empty container through which God could transform my very being.

After many weeks of just showing up, I began to notice subtle changes, almost imperceptible differences that no one would have noticed except me. A different way of responding, perhaps. A little more patience, a little less judgment, more genuine feelings of compassion. Not a major spiritual overhaul, but slight changes, nonetheless. My exterior behavior seemed to be silently supported from the inside out—oh so slowly.

But it wasn't all roses and light. Along with the budding signs of fruits of the spirit, God also began to reveal truths about my real motives, my hidden agendas, my shadow traits. The unveiled self-deceptions seemed so appalling that I wanted to turn back to unconsciousness, but it was impossible. The knowledge tumbling out of Pandora's box couldn't be stuffed back in, even though some of it was not pretty.

Ultimately, I came to accept this blind light of reality as part of God's formative process, encompassed not by judgment and shame, but by forgiveness and acceptance. I also became grateful that in God's infinite mercy, I was only shown one thing at a time! Without *my* management and effort—just as in that still winter garden—growth was somehow being accomplished. I allowed the silence to turn from adversary to advisor, from foe to friend. I experienced it as a place of open vulnerability that became more and more trustworthy.

Rather than inverting a life of service into mere navel-gazing, silence and solitude can be a place where one's spiritual engine is charged and set into motion. Unless one is able to sit quietly, enduring the clamor of competing voices in the psyche, one can never learn to distinguish the still small voice of God from the noisy chorus. Silence practice is far from lazy inactivity. It can be the most transformative work imaginable, sending the person into the world as a channel of love. It's a lifetime endeavor, to be sure, but it begins with that first step into the silence.

"Salvation Means Security"

It seems to me that sometimes Christian language about salvation is little more than thinly disguised narcissism. At its root, it is often about satisfying our own desires and getting what we want. How can I get to heaven? How many stars will be in my crown? How can I get my prayers answered? How can I garner more blessings? How I can get God to give me what I want? This is a far cry from the centrality of selfless love that Jesus embodied and proclaimed. Beware of self-interest disguised as piety and goodness.

This ego-centered perspective is a wolf in sheep's clothing that appeals to some of our most basic neediness—to be rewarded and protected from harm. When the psalmist sang praises to God as "my light and my salvation" (Ps 27:1) or when the writer of Philippians urged Christians to "work out your own salvation with fear and trembling" (Phil 2:12), more is implied than securing a spot in paradise or an invisible buffer against pain and hardship. Surely, salvation calls us to a process of drawing closer to the Source of All, a God whose very character is love (1 John 4). We can grow toward loving and honoring God for God-*self*, rather than for what we can get out of it. We spend a lifetime living out the implications of that journey into the meaning and wholeness that we call salvation—a process designed to save us from our ego-dominated selves.

Hear the words of Reverend Steve Garnas-Holmes: "When we turn to God, it is so often for what we want to receive. 'Give me peace.' 'Give me healing' 'Give me faith.' But true love is for the sake of the beloved. To love God is not to demand God's devotion, but to give God our own."[13]

So, our ways of *seeing*—our perspectives—determine the direction of our energy and to some extent the course of our lives.

- When our focus is on the *past*, our energy dissipates into what was, what could have been.

- When our focus is on the *future*, our energy is invested in what ought to be, what might be.

- When our focus is on the *present*, our energy is concentrated into an acceptance of what is.

And that brings us to our next group of blockades to freedom—our persistent patterns.

For Reflection

1. Did you grow up with an image of a demanding God who wanted you to "get it right?" How has that affected your religious faith?

2. How do you experience the difference between flexibility and adaptation? To what extent do you rely on others to tell you who you are?

3. What perspective seems to be thwarting or distorting your spiritual journey? Is there a belief that keeps tripping you up?

Letting Go of Patterns

A soft answer turns away wrath, but a harsh word stirs up anger. (Prov 15:1)

"Why does that always set me off?" Laura asked, as she described the discussion that erupted in a burst of temper. Some innocent statement, some familiar situation had ignited a whole set of predictable responses. And the downward spiral began. And to think it had started with a simple question, "Isn't supper ready yet?"

Somewhere "once upon a time" we developed ways of acting and reacting that became entrenched—grooved into our psyches and spirits in ways that put our behavior on automatic pilot. Unless we uncover our particular pathways and summon the courage to let the harmful behaviors go, we are destined to repeat the same old cycles that prevent our progress.

Psychology tells us that insanity is repeating the same behavior and expecting the results to change. Most patterns started out innocently and unconsciously, in the service of our emotional survival as children. Mostly, we did the best we could, behaving in ways that we hoped would protect us from pain and gain us love when other methods didn't seem to work. So we regress into those immature patterns over and over again—until we decide to take a deep breath and examine them.

As I think back to the Christmas scene in the motel room that I described in chapter 1, I can see the re-enactment of a long-established pattern of mine—figure it out, grit your teeth, make a list, and get cranking. Make it better—you can do it if you really try. And keep smiling. Not a bad pattern, you might say, except that it covered a well of unspeakable sadness and unhealed wounds that have taken years to integrate. And that was only the tip of the iceberg.

Even as I determined to face my feelings with the help of a professional, the old pattern continued to sabotage me. In the midst of a session involving an emotional trauma, my counselor casually asked me, "So how did that *feel* to you?" I launched into a lengthy description of the feelings when suddenly she held up her hand to stop me, saying, "Linda, do you realize that you *talk* about your feelings, rather than *feeling* them? You *think* about them; you don't *experience* them. There's a total disconnect. When you get close to a painful place, you go straight to your thinking function—analyzing it and masking it over with words. From now on, when you go to your head, I'm not going with you!" At the moment, I had no idea what she meant. But her confrontation cracked open the protective shell around my locked-away wounds, leading the way to some serious healing work.

To tell the truth, I still like to make a list and get cranking—it's in my hard-wiring. And I'm still an extroverted wordsmith who likes to figure things out. However, these days I try consciously to use the behaviors rather than letting the behaviors use me. And when I smile, it's more likely to reflect joy rather than determination. I try to remember that negativity poisons our thoughts; we need to drop it like a hot coal.

To find out what patterns are in place, it helps to listen to the voices in your head. What recurrent phrases do you use? How do you talk to yourself? What behaviors seem to take you over for no justifiable reason? Here are a few examples to nudge you down your personal path of patterns.

"Yes, but . . ."

"Yes, but they might get mad at me."

"Yes, but I don't have time."

"Yes, but they shouldn't have done that."

One day I heard a kindergarten teacher playfully chastise her class by saying "I'm tired of hearing 'yes, but.' Anything followed by 'but' is just an excuse; I'm going to have to put you on 'but' restriction!" When the class erupted in hilarity, she knew she had found a humorous way to instill a deeper truth. On this road to letting go, we too may need to "restrict our 'buts.'"

A phrase beginning with "but" is like putting the brakes on a moving car, slowing it down, breaking its momentum, keeping it from reaching its destination. Though it sometimes introduces an important exception or a warning, most of the time it's an excuse not to move ahead into uncharted territory. In other words, it's used in the service of our fear and timidity to keep from taking a risk.

Every time my friend Greg reaches a point of taking responsibility for his own growth, he lapses into "yes, but." I can see it coming as he sighs and repeats, "Yes, but that's the way I was brought up. That's just the way I am." Then once again he detours away from his own soul into the sins of his family of origin, getting bogged down in the blame-game. To be sure, those issues must be pursued and felt deeply; we can't let go of something we haven't really felt. However, many people choose to remain in the cycle of "yes, but" long after those feelings have been explored, thereby putting the brakes on their journey to wholeness. And they often get stuck there, mired in their own woundedness.

In a similar way, Celeste bemoans her repeated relationship failures, automatically assuming that others will reject and exclude her. "Yes, but I can't join that group. They won't like me." "Yes, but I 'm afraid to visit that church—no one will talk to me." Her deep fear of abandonment gets projected on to others, so long as she refuses to deal with her own issues. The first step toward dismantling these patterns is taking responsibility for them.

The "yes, but" kind of pessimism spreads its toxic tentacles into every aspect of life. It engages the familiar metaphor of the half-empty cup, when we ignore the reality that the cup is also half-full. "Yes, but" behaves like a low-grade depression that throws a gray blanket over everything, dimming the radiance of relationships, work, physical health. Nothing escapes its murkiness. We see the world through a pair of gray-tinted glasses. In letting go of these negative patterns, we must have the courage to affirm that the gray blanket is *ours*; the dark glasses are *ours*. This can be tedious inner work, but there's a liberating payoff in the sense of buoyancy and freedom that will begin to form.

Letting go of negativity is a choice, but not an easy one. Our sense of self can become attached to the excuses and intertwined with cynicism.

- Try to catch yourself complaining. Listen for "Yes, but . . ."

- Allow a blinking red light to begin flashing in your spirit, warning "Stop!" when negative chatter creeps in.

- Notice the nature of your inner dialogue.

- Monitor the messages you constantly give yourself. Are they self-deprecating? Is your interior voice (the "critical mother") working overtime? It's time to fire her!

The old adage warns us, "All the water in the world cannot sink a ship unless it gets inside." When negative voices—someone else's or our own—get inside our psychic "ships," taking over the helm, we can count on a shipwreck.

Another sign of "yes, but" thinking lurks behind statements such as "I know you must think I'm stupid, but. . . ," or "I'm sure you think this house is a mess, but. . ." This pattern is an unconscious projection of your own inner self-criticism onto others by assuming you know what they think. Again, become aware of the phrases and thoughts that are built on a negative foundation.

Obviously, we want to change our "yes, buts" to a resounding *yes*, removing the backdoor barricades that block our path. That can't happen until we discern the patterns that stand in our way, connect the dots to the inner core of wounding, and begin to release them. We can say compassionately to that wounded inner child, "I know why you're feeling this negative outburst, this recurrent pain. I know how you ended up like this, but I'm choosing not to run this pattern again."

Hear the words of Dawna Markova in *I Will Not Die An Unlived Life*: "All around me, the aspen trees are shedding their dried golden leaves. I need to shed, to let go of what no longer is alive, to get bare enough to find the bones of what is important to me. I need to let go of the ways of knowing that have not, cannot, and will not take me where I want to go."[1]

"What's Wrong With Me?"

Joyce's morning devotional routine was as precise and punctual as she was. She lit a candle, said her rosary, studied the saints, and prayed fervently on her knees. The presence of God was vivid and enriching during these early-morning moments.

And then it wasn't. Dryness and boredom set in. She was restless, distracted, following the rabbit trails of her wandering mind. "What's wrong with me?" she asked. "It isn't like it used to be. I feel so guilty and disobedient. I know what God expects of me; and I'm not being obedient."

"Are you sure you know?" I replied. "Maybe this is the Spirit's way of leading you to a different kind of relationship, a new way of praying. Maybe this restlessness is a sign of God's leading, not a condemnation. If we didn't experience dis-ease, we would never ever change. Maybe it's divine discontent!"

Joyce decided to dismiss her own judgments and projections and pray through the discontent, asking God to reveal unexplored methods of connecting to the sacred. First, she tried to be open to her *natural* ways of feeling and expressing. She began to incorporate prayer into her walking routine. An avid nature-lover, she began to seek God in the sounds, sights, and smells of creation. Her daily gardening began to burst with meaning as the task of seed-planting, watering, and blossoming became metaphors for the movement of God's spirit in her life. These fresh approaches breathed new energy into her spiritual journey.

Still the guilt remained. The fear of divine displeasure kept returning. Finally another light bulb came on, as she realized that her own belief in God as stern judge was constricting her spirit. She had to let that image go in order to relate to God as enlivening joy. She embraced this new pattern of openness, and spiritual freedom began to flourish.

Predictably, loosening her demanding grip on herself had a surprising domino effect. She naturally became less exacting and legalistic with her family and friends. As she let go of her automatic self-blame, she realized that what she thought was *wrong* with her was actually *right* with her—all a part of her journey to authenticity.

"It Isn't Fair!"

For I envied the arrogant when I saw the prosperity of the wicked. They have no struggles; their bodies are healthy and strong. They are free from the burdens common to man; they are not plagued by human ills . . . This is what the wicked are like—always carefree, they increase in wealth. (Ps 73:4, 5, 12, NIV)

Just tune in to the conversation of a group of toddlers and you'll hear, "His cookie is bigger than mine!" "I had it first!" "It just isn't fair!" But the outrage isn't confined to children. Our grown-up words are similar, "Life just shouldn't *be* like that!"

We seem to be created with a desire for fairness and balance. From the trivial to the terrible, we want life to make sense—for vice to be punished and virtue to be rewarded. Whether it's a chocolate pie or the mythical American Pie, our innate sense of justice demands that everyone have an equal slice.

Most of us grew up with an idea called the "theory of divine retribution": do good and you will be blessed; obey God's laws and you will prosper. So what do we do with the inequities that are all around us? Life experience has a way of shattering our illusions about everyone getting a fair shake. We see children suffering, we see greed being exalted, and it seems that simple justice is a mystery at best, a fantasy at worst. And the resulting bewilderment and frustration can stop us dead in our spiritual tracks.

When life fails to measure up to this logical standard, how can we deal with our confusion? Jesus' words about the inverted values of the kingdom may appear to add to the perplexity. From the parable of the Good Samaritan to the experience of the cross, this world's values and expectations are turned upside-down. Perhaps instead, Scripture calls us to a new understanding of the mystery of fairness and the necessity for trust in some sort of divine justice, though it may be incomprehensible to us in this life.

Hear Jesus' parable of the laborers in the vineyard:

> For the kingdom of heaven is like a landowner who went out early in the morning to hire laborers for his vineyard. After agreeing with the laborers for the usual daily wage, he sent them into his vineyard. When he went out about nine o'clock, he saw others standing idle in the marketplace; and he said to them, "You also go into the vineyard, and I will pay you whatever is right." So they went. When he went out again about noon and about three o'clock, he did the same. And about five o'clock he went out and found others standing around; and he said to them, "Why are you standing here idle all day?" They said to him, "Because no one has hired us." He said to them, "You also go into the vineyard." When evening came, the owner of the vineyard said to his manager, "Call the laborers and give them their pay, beginning with the last and then going to the first." When those hired about five o'clock came, each of them received the usual daily wage. Now when the first came, they thought they would receive more; but each of them also received the usual daily wage. And when they received it, they grumbled against the landowner, saying, "These last worked only one hour, and you have made them equal to us who have borne the burden of the day and the scorching heat." But he replied to one of them, "Friend, I am doing you no wrong; did you not agree with me for the usual daily wage? Take what belongs to you and go; I choose to give to this last the same as I give to you. Am I not allowed to do what I choose with what belongs to me? Or are you

envious because I am generous?" So the last will be first, and the first will be last. (Matt 20:1–16)

Paying those who sweated all day in the sun the same as the ones who worked one hour? Clearly, this unfair arrangement could not be tolerated in corporate America! Jesus is not suggesting a new economic order, but rather making a graphic point about the mysterious values of the kingdom of God and the lavish generosity of the landowner.

What about the story of the lost sheep? Leave ninety-nine sheep in jeopardy while you search for one that is lost? Hardly cost effective by business measurements. Further still, consider the parable of the Good Samaritan, where the hero of the story is a social outcast of the culture. Yet he was illogically portrayed as good—again a reversal of society's standards. Ditto for the Prodigal Son, where, not only did the young man *not* receive the punishment he deserved, but was welcomed with a lavish gala, thrown in his honor.

Jesus insists that, in the spiritual realm, there is a kind of justice that transcends our contemporary notions of square deals and fair play. Our cultural conditioning and human standards of fairness may be understandable in running a civilized society. But if we seek to impose them on the kingdom of God, they just won't fit.

Let's move to the flesh-and-blood arena of our human experience. Letting go of our preconceived notions of fairness sometimes requires all the faith we can muster when tragic circumstances move us from the abstract to the very, very real. My friend Caroline is the ideal grandmother—vibrant, creative, devout—doting on her precious first grandchild, Davey. When signs of a debilitating genetic disorder began to appear in the child, the family's denial and disbelief soon turned to gut-wrenching grief. Every medical solution was sought; endless prayers were prayed. The future held a bleak forecast of deterioration and a shortened lifespan.

Caroline had been through hard times before—the traumatic death of a sibling in her childhood and her own bout with cancer, sadly preparing her for this ultimate challenge to fairness and faith. She opened herself to the tragic realities of families throughout the world, claiming a perspective that changed the question "Why us?" to "Why not us?" With the support of a caring community of friends and a deep trust in God's goodness, she began to find ways to use her sorrows.

"I've had to let go of Davey's future," she mused. "There's a huge freedom in that, strangely enough. I no longer worry about what he's going to be or whether he'll get accepted to Harvard. He's free to be completely himself, to live noncompetitively in our eyes."

Step by painful step, she came to a creative acceptance of the situation, making every moment with Davey a celebration, seeing his short life as an immense gift. "I polish every moment as brightly as I can," she remarked with a smile. "When I am with Davey, I smell him; I savor the texture of his skin; I find joy in everything he does and says. He has an incredible gift for bringing people together, as if he were on a mission of love and reconciliation."

As the family has begun to treasure Davey's presence in their lives, he has become a point of light and healing for others. Caroline's bedrock belief in the mystery of grace was stronger than her need for fairness.

"I'm Worried Sick"

> So do not worry about tomorrow, for tomorrow will bring worries of its own. Today's trouble is enough for today. (Matt 6:34)

> And can any of you by worrying add a single hour to your span of life? (Matt 6:27)

It's difficult to make a good case for the practice of worrying, though in my family of origin, everybody tried. The women had a way of equating worry with love, and I soon learned to translate their particular language of affection.

"I've been lying awake all night worrying about you! You can't imagine how I worry," was a frequent refrain. So it is in many families. From early on, many of us get the message that worrying is a virtue, a sign that one cares deeply. In my family it was never actually spoken, mind you, but it was clear that the greater the worry, the greater the love.

Not only does worry obscure the language of love, not only is it unscriptural, but it's even bad for our health. Studies show that people age more by worry than by work. Worry fatigues the brain and sabotages creative and constructive thought. It constricts the muscles and inhibits blood flow. It seems to gain a life of its own, repeating the toxic mental pictures that continue to cause pain and consternation. In other words, it makes you *sick*. I don't mean to be glib about a truly serious matter, because obviously there is much in this world to worry about. It just doesn't do any *good*. As the old saying goes, "Worry is like a rocking chair; it gives you something to do, but it doesn't get you anywhere."

Part of our difficulty, it seems, comes from our failure to distinguish between fruitless worry and appropriate concern. Much of the time, failure to worry *feels* irresponsible, irrational, even neglectful. I remember my own parental fears of my child running into the street, falling from a tree limb, getting behind the wheel of a car. Prudence dictates some preventive action—knowledge of safety rules, driving lessons—but hand-wringing anticipation of disaster accomplishes nothing but ulcers. And it absolutely, positively robs us of the joy of the moment, peppering our thoughts and speech with those telltale words, "What if," and "Watch out! You might hurt yourself." There will always be a healthy tension between trust and responsibility. After all, we seek to trust God with our children's safety, but we don't leave a three-year old at home unattended.

When we feel we have taken responsible precautions in a situation, faced a dilemma squarely and wisely, then it's time to nip worry in the bud. After all, worry is essentially a habit, and like other bad habits, it should be replaced by a good habit, one that engages positive energy. (Special techniques for this will be mentioned in part 3.) But, before we can undertake replacement remedies, we must become aware of our own patterns of worry.

Notice your preoccupations, and learn to discern when appropriate concern bleeds over into stifling worry. Do your legitimate health concerns consume an inordinate amount of your time and energy? Do you fret excessively about the ups and downs of your financial condition? Do you restrict your activities because of unfounded fears? Do you spend time spinning theoretical scenarios about what *might* happen? As the old saying goes, "Today is the tomorrow you worried about yesterday, and all is well."

Spiritually speaking, worry and faith are just plain incompatible. Worry tends to form thoughts of fear or blame; faith forms thoughts of acceptance and gratitude. Physically speaking, worry brings tension; faith brings relaxation. What better reasons do we need for letting this pattern go?

I suppose a little humor always helps. The brilliant Charles Schultz wrote: "Don't worry about the world coming to an end. It's already tomorrow in Australia!"

"I Am So Upset. . ."

Be angry but do not sin; do not let the sun go down on your anger . . . (Eph 4:26)

You do well to be angry—but don't use your anger as fuel for revenge. (Eph 4:26)[2]

A soft answer turns away wrath, but a harsh word stirs up anger. (Prov 15:1)

Refrain from anger, and forsake wrath. Do not fret—it leads only to evil. (Ps 37:8)

"Of course I've forgiven him," she emphasized, with a look of self-righteousness. "Besides, God will take care of it for me!" Judy's bitterness was palpable, but she couldn't see it through her fog of Christian conviction. She had survived the messy, embarrassing divorce from a philandering husband, and had convinced herself that she had "complied" with what she viewed as the requirements of her religion. All she had really done was transfer her need for revenge to the fiery judgment of God—or, at least, the God she imagined.

When it comes to judgmentalism, blame, anger, and resentment, human beings seem honor bound to justify their feelings and nurture them in every way possible. It reminds me of scratching a raging case of poison ivy—it feels so good to scratch it, but all it does is spread the poison. As we "scratch" these negative feelings by thinking them to death and describing them in repeated episodes, they naturally become angrier and darker. We'll just call one more person to tell them what happened; we'll plan all the things we might say at our next encounter with the offender and imagine the response, we'll . . . and the toxic feelings do their dirty work, both in our bodies and in our relationships. They take on a life of their own, and they often won't rest until we take some aggressive action.

Frederick Buechner's graphic description certainly got my attention:

> Of the Seven Deadly Sins, anger is possibly the most fun. To lick your wounds, to smack your lips over grievances long past, to roll over your tongue the prospect of bitter confrontations still to come, to savor to the last toothsome morsel both the pain you are given and the pain you are giving back—in many ways it is a feast fit for a king. The chief drawback is that what you are wolfing down is *yourself.* The skeleton at the feast is *you.*[3]

The medical evidence is that this scary scenario is almost literally true. Studies are piling up that catalog the physical consequences of habitual anger—tension headaches, stomach upset, muscle constriction, high blood pressure, and a host of other very *real* and damaging ailments. It's as if we're drinking poison and expecting someone else to get sick! The price we pay for our complicity in feeding this negative energy is not only diminished health, but also chronic unhappiness.

Anger is a wicked warlord if it gets in charge. Though this natural emotion can be a rich source of information for us, it's our task to make it our servant rather than our master. Julia Cameron in *The Artist's Way* wrote some memorable words about anger: "Anger is meant to be listened to. Anger is a voice, a shout, a plea, a demand. Anger is meant to be respected. Why? Because anger is a map. Anger shows us what our boundaries are. Anger is meant to be acted upon. It is *not* meant to be acted out."[4]

We can allow it to provide vital self-knowledge by pausing to ask some pointed questions: What in me is activated? Fear of disapproval or abandonment? Evidence of some unhealed wound from way back? Those angry places inside us need to be recognized, listened to, felt, and accepted—without judgment. Only then can the healing begin. We can't let go of something we haven't felt and owned.

But let's not railroad over the feeling and listening part of this emotional equation, because anger always has something important to teach us. It tells us that something is amiss; something needs to change. Feel the pain or guilt in your body, and ask it what it wants. Believe it or not, you can make it your friend and your ally in your own growth.

Have the courage to focus on your response rather than the other person's behavior—which you can't change anyway. Deciding to let go of this poisonous merry-go-round takes some clear thinking, devoid of emotional heat. So, taking a few deep breaths and deliberately gaining some emotional distance is key. A basic and necessary realization is that letting go of anger is not condoning bad behavior. It means that you make a conscious decision that you no longer want to harbor the negative energy that robs you of joy. You want to be *rid of it*. That involves confronting the feelings and making responsible choices about how to react. Then, for the sake of spiritual, emotional, and physical health, release the feelings. (Tools to engage the process of forgiveness will be discussed in the "How" section of this book.)

The pattern of blaming—others or ourselves—is another dead-end behavior that dissipates our power to deal with our own growth. So long as we conveniently shift the blame for all the world's ills, as well as our own circumstances, onto other individuals or groups, we can temporarily let ourselves off the hook. This keeps us from asking responsible questions, such as:

"What can I do to make our community schools better, rather than engaging in this constant complaining?"

"How can I set proper boundaries, rather than grumble about the incursion of others into my time and space?"

"What steps can I take to deal with the pain of that trauma so that I'll be in a position to release it?"

"Are there ways I can contribute to the political process instead of merely whining about it?"

Even more insidious, however, is the underlying pattern of judgmentalism that masks as discernment. We make divisive statements like, "I have to stand up against their evil," or repeat ethnic humor, "Have you heard the one about. . . ?" or foster our competitive spirits, "God is on our side and will lead us to victory." Sadly, many human beings have a tendency to spend their lives in an attitude of competition rather than cooperation.

Evaluating a situation to make a wise response is different than indulging in a knee-jerk reaction that condemns others as unworthy or immoral or stupid. Every time we make a derogatory statement about another, a warning bell should sound in our souls, alerting us that there is something inside us that needs to belittle another in order to elevate ourselves. In other words, when we judge another, we don't define them so much as we define ourselves as *one who needs to judge*. In reality, our actions and our words judge *us*.

"This Will Make Me Feel Better. . ."

Most of us have a low tolerance for pain. Whether it's a headache or a heartache, we want something to make it better—right now. The capacity to ride the crest of pain or to just hang in there is anti-cultural.

In his groundbreaking book, *Addiction and Grace*, Dr. Gerald May stretched the boundaries of my ideas about addiction. Most of us point at alcohol and drugs as addictive habits and fail to see the same pattern of destructive behavior in attachments to power, people, work, intimacy, and an endless list of obsessions. Consider the familiar example of the derelict who loses everything in his life as alcohol becomes the controlling force. But right around the corner may be a man in a three-piece suit, a model citizen, who is consumed with the next business deal, devoted to material success at the expense of his personal relationships. Or the wife who is addicted to an abusive husband, whom she is powerless to leave.

Dr. May asserts that our deepest desire is to experience the love of God, whether we use those terms or not. "Our creation is by love, in love, and for love," he writes. But our free will chooses various forms of addiction, which become the objects of our time and energy, instead of love. May identifies the main carriers of addiction in our culture: ". . . the three gods we do trust for security are possessions, power, and human relationships. To a greater or lesser extent, all of us worship this false trinity."[5]

Before we can let go of patterns that retard our growth, we must first identify what they are. Spend some time looking honestly at the things that command your thoughts and drive your decisions. To what do you naturally turn when you want to feel better? Does food occupy too much of your attention? Do you retreat to mindless TV to anesthetize your discomfort? Are you consumed with compulsive cleanliness or neatness? Shopping sprees to lift your spirits? A bigger and better house? More luxurious trips? A new romance? Since these addictions don't carry the social stigma of drugs and alcohol, we often fail to see the ways they usurp our journey to wholeness.

"When This Is Over"

I heard myself muttering again, "Just a few more days from now this will be *over*." I was eager to get the week behind me, even though I was knee-deep in a project that I was supposed to be enjoying. And I wasn't the only one. I could hear the recurrent strains in the comments of my friends, "When I lose weight . . . When I find Mr. Right . . . When the kids are grown . . . When I can retire . . . When the loan is paid off . . ." I could hear my mother's voice echoing from the past, "You're wishing your life away!"

Then another recent memory poked me in the psychological ribs. At the theater a few weeks before, I recalled my customary antsy-ness, as I repeatedly checked the playbook to see when the curtain would come down and how I could sneak to the nearest exit before the aisles crowded. Never mind that I had relished the review and paid big bucks for the orchestra seats. Mentally, my pattern was one of standing in some imaginary queue, tapping my foot.

All my dependable defenses began their customary march forward. My schedule was too full; I had to learn to say no; I needed to do things I truly enjoyed. But I sensed something larger at work, like a familiar tape playing, a pattern of impatient projection. I would often get up in the morning, already looking forward to the evening let-down that I associated with the six o'clock news on TV. Gradually, I began to realize that the edgy pattern would often weave itself through my entire day. Besides clouding my focus and jerking me off-center, it was literally robbing me of the joy of the moment. This way of ticking off the minutes—eyes cast ahead and body leaning forward—can become the modus operandi of curious, busy people whose calendars are cluttered not only with what they *must* do, but also with what they *want* to do. There's work to do; there are books to read, people to help, prayers to pray, mountains to climb, seas to sail, good deeds to be done. And, regrettably, the good is often the enemy of the best. Time needed to pursue a higher calling can get gobbled up by a host of worthwhile endeavors.

As with most habitual patterns, this way of being offers daunting challenges. For one thing, it usually masquerades as efficiency—a much-admired attribute in our culture. And it's largely unconscious—nobody ever says, "I think I'll take my mind and energy elsewhere while this wonderful thing is going on right in front of me." Or "Even though I've told myself I want to be right here, 75% of me has already moved on to the next thing." Of course not. If this is your pattern, you do it without even thinking about it. Operating on automatic pilot, these behaviors bypass your decision-making mechanisms.

Projecting ahead may be useful when you're poised for serious surgery or need to use spare time to outline a plan, but not when it becomes a daily pattern. When I misplaced my day-planner for a *whole day* last week, I felt as if a part of me had been amputated. It was a blinking red light that reminded me of writer Sara Ban Breathnach's clever and quotable reference to ". . . the woman still clutching the To Do list underneath her straitjacket . . ." in her book *Romancing the Ordinary*.[6] Surely there must be a happy medium between comfortable organization that smooths out the day and the paranoid planning that usurps spontaneity.

Don't get me wrong—I guess I will always be a recovering multi-tasker. I may continue to empty the dishwasher and water the plants while I'm talking on the phone, but my compulsion to be perpetually busy deserves a withering look. In fact, I'm beginning to think that my devotion to productivity is counter-productive to my soul's serenity—a pattern that needs to be changed. Later in the book, we'll explore specific ways to invest ourselves more fully in the present.

"I Can't Throw That Away!"

Janice had just completed a long-postponed project—she had cleaned out her closets. The clutter had been reduced, unused items sent to charity organizations to give to the needy. She had retained only the things she needed or the things she was lovingly attached to. Surprisingly, she was noticing an inner clean-up as well, with feelings of serenity and simplicity. In other words, she was discovering that there was a correlation between her external clutter and her internal chaos.

I know a married couple to whom this kind of letting go can set off a third world war. One is a packrat, the other a neatnik, so you can only imagine the charged atmosphere when it's time to clean out the garage. They came up with a list of useful questions to consider when deciding what to let go:

Do I love it?

Do I need it?

Does it support who I am now in my life?

Does it act as an environmental affirmation for me?

What positive or negative thoughts, memories, or emotions do I associate with it?

Does it need to be fixed or repaired, and am I willing to do so *now*?

If it's time to let it go, am I going to sell, lend, or give it away—and *when*?

How often have you heard yourself say, "I need to simplify my life"? The deep process of letting go involves not only clearing our cluttered space, but also dealing with our cluttered schedules, cluttered thoughts, and cluttered spirits. And that kind of inner and outer "housecleaning" means more than straightening that junky kitchen drawer beside the telephone or unraveling the tangle of computer cords on the floor.

It keeps occurring to me as I observe my own life and the lives of others that we often miss the kingdom, rush right past the abundant life, and put our own souls in jeopardy because we live such hurried, noisy lives. In fact, the recurrent refrain that I hear from most folks is "I am just sooooo busy. I can't seem to get everything done . . . there aren't enough hours in the day." Sound familiar?

This harried attitude is an equal opportunity employer—it rules people, regardless of race, creed, or national origin. From doctors to ditch-diggers, life piles endlessly upon itself until the beautiful experience of being alive melts into one enormous *obligation*, leaving us exhausted and stripped of joy. The truth is, there is often a hidden psychological payoff to our claim to busyness. Our culture rewards it, for one thing, but there's another underlying motivation that bears scrutiny. We proclaim this "busyness" to one another with some hidden degree of pride, as if our exhaustion were a trophy, our ability to withstand stress a mark of real character. The busier we are, the more important we seem to ourselves and—we think—to others. Unfortunately, this has become the model of a successful life.

Our lives are so crammed full of things, people, projects, and schedules that a familiar bumper sticker becomes true for us: "Life is what happens to us while we're making other plans." We fail to be totally present to this adventure called life.

The world's major religious traditions point to this need to simplify, simplify, simplify. The yearning of our souls concurs. Yet this higher wisdom runs smack into the cultural message that says "produce" and "possess." Regardless of what we say, when we take a close look at what we do—how we actually spend our money and time—it appears we've bought into that flawed notion. What we produce and possess is society's measure of our worth, and unconsciously, we usually apply that measuring stick to ourselves and to others.

As we ascend the ladder of success, we begin to accumulate and stockpile, plunging us into the slippery slope of production, possession, and pursuit of pleasure. This starts eating up our time and money, until our planned purchases, our planned trips, and our planned activities begin to drive all our decisions. Before we know it, our lives are cluttered with the *maintenance* of all this stuff we've acquired and the lifestyle we've enshrined. What a vicious cycle!

What about our spiritual clutter? "Be still, and know that I am God," says Ps 46:10. It doesn't say, "Read another book and you'll know; tackle another worthy project and you'll know, or even study the Bible and you'll know." It says to be still—silent, motionless, uncluttered.

Obviously, the problem of clutter in our lives isn't confined to the back hall closet that we hope no one will open. Our time has a clutter problem, too. Periodically, most busy people exclaim, "Something's got to go!" Examining a packed schedule can be a challenge, but the familiar Parable of the Rocks offers a wise starting point:

> A professor stood before his Time Management class with an object lesson. He picked up a gallon-sized glass jar and began to fill it with fist-sized rocks, then asked the class, "Is the jar full?" They all answered yes. Then he reached for a bucket of gravel and poured it into the jar, allowing the smaller rocks to settle around the larger ones. Again he asked, "Is the jar full?" And again, they replied with a resounding yes. He then produced a container of sand, which he added to the jar, and it filled in the empty spaces. Again the same question, "Is it full?" This time, only a few said yes. Finally, he brought in a pitcher of water, which indeed did fill the jar to the brim. His demonstration completed, he asked his class, "Now what is the moral of this story?" A clever student immediately raised his hand and proclaimed proudly, "The point of the story is that no matter how much you have to do, you can always fit something else in!" "No," the professor replied. "The moral of the story is that if you don't put your big rocks in first, you'll never get them in at all."

In deciding what our "big rocks" are, we're likely to let some other things go, at least for a while. Of course, our priorities are constantly changing as our lives evolve. Tasks like child care, tending a sick family member, starting a new business, completing an important project—can occupy prime space in our lives for a time. However, if we prayerfully keep our deepest values in view—those of loving God with our heart, soul, mind, and strength and our neighbors as ourselves, we are more likely to parcel out our time and energy prudently.

At any given time, there are things that only we can do, things that others can do, and things we can put off until later. Wise teacher Flora Wuellner taught that there is a significant difference between seeing what needs to be done and being called to do it. There are many worthwhile tasks to undertake. If what you're doing has an underlying sense of joy and fulfillment, it's probably yours to do. If, on the other hand, that joy is missing and you have a feeling of constant drudgery, then you've probably picked up someone else's cross. Letting go of unnecessary activity is a vital part of clearing our clutter.

However, at the base of all the hoarding and grasping, the cluttering of our space and our spirits, lies the pattern of filling our lives to the brim, leaving little room for our soul's life with God. Those who minister to dying persons have said that no one ever wishes they had purchased more stuff at the end of their lives, nor do they wish they had spent more time at the office. They're more likely to feel, "Did I love enough? Did I give enough? Am I going to die with my music still in me?"

Identifying our patterns of clutter usually nudges us toward simplicity in all its forms. And simple moments, I have found, are usually introduced to us through the eyes of children and nature. I was reminded of this during a memorable morning stroll with my young grandson along the Spring River in Arkansas. We were meandering along the river path when Andrew stopped abruptly in his tracks.

"Lindy!" he gasped. "What is *that*?"

He was face-to-face with a spectacular spider web, stretching precariously across the path from bush to bush, its precision outlined in sparkling dewdrops.

"Wow. This is the special work of the spider," I said, as we examined the pattern that looked like a piece of Victorian lace.

"The spider's special task is to climb the branch, release the tiny silk thread from her body, and cast it into space," I explained to Andrew. "She trusts that it will 'catch' somewhere so that she can begin her work. Then she connects one silk thread to another, making a beautiful pattern. And when that pattern isn't needed any more, she must let it go and start another pattern."

Andrew kept staring—and thinking this over. Then he asked, "But how does she know how to do it?"

"Well," I said, "somehow God made her with special knowledge inside of her and when she listens to it, she knows it will guide her. God creates us with everything we need."

Of course, I couldn't help making my own connections. I thought about how much we risk when we open our lives to God in trust. We, too, take a leap of faith. We willingly enter a complex process, one spiritual step at a time, and trust that new patterns will form. And, like the spider, we must sometimes let those patterns go and risk ourselves again in the light of God's grace, weaving the next pattern of meaning into our web of days. Who would have thought we could have so much in common with a lowly spider?

As you explore the patterns of your own life, remember that the same loving guidance that inspires the spider's journey of letting go can also inspire your own.

For Reflection

1. Which of these patterns seems to be the most prevalent in your life experience? Can you name the sources of these repeated behaviors?

2. Examine the questions posed in the section on anger ("I Am So Upset"). Answer them as honestly as you can. What is your anger teaching you?

3. What are your major sources of worry? What can be done to convert pointless worries into constructive caution?

4. Is your external clutter resulting in internal confusion? What steps are you willing to take to alleviate that situation?

Letting Go of Plans

Do not remember the former things, or consider the things of old. I am about to do a new thing; now it springs forth, do you not perceive it? (Isa 43:18, 19)

"Set goals."
"Be the captain of your ship."
"Control your life."
"Make a plan."

Sounds like good advice. And it is, if you're opening a new business. But in the business of letting go, making plans may be part of the problem, not the solution. The act of letting go calls for relinquishing some of your plans—the rigid agendas and unspoken dreams that can prevent you from being open to God's best for you. And that means looking beneath your surface actions and recognizing your compulsion to control.

Few actions are more unsettling than approaching the subject of surrender. The very word itself can conjure up images of a defeated soldier waving a white flag—helpless, vulnerable, out of control. No wonder it can strike fear in our hearts. But the truth of surrender is much more about saying "Yes!" than "I give up."

One day Maria arrived for her monthly spiritual direction appointment without her notebook. Usually she had a neat page of "spiritual issues" and a pen in hand poised to make necessary notes. A very successful business woman, she was prepared, prompt, and proactive. But today, she seemed a bit disconnected, unsure of herself. Something was clearly different, and I wondered what was going on.

Her first words were a tip-off, "Well, I don't really know what to talk about today—I don't have any plans for our session. Maybe I shouldn't even have come." She sounded as if she were in uncomfortable territory without her agenda. I decided to explore the transition and suggested a time of quiet, listening prayer, hoping that we could both get out of the way and allow the Spirit to lead the session.

After the silence settled over us, we chatted companionably. It wasn't long before little bits of conversation yielded clues. First, she began venting about some unexplored tension with a co-worker. Her words showed a willingness to consider *her own* reactions. "I wonder what's causing this feeling of competition and envy inside me," she remarked. Other latent feelings began to slowly bubble up, unbidden—financial concerns, signs of stress, time constraints. In each instance, there was a minimum of blame and a tendency to tackle probing questions about her own motives. She was searching for meaning. For a long time, the talk seemed aimless and meandering, but I trusted that some important connections were forming.

Finally, I ventured a guess. "It sounds as if your soul is trying to move toward integration, Maria. Your spiritual life and your corporate life are one life, and your soul seems to be straining toward unity. It wants to explore the gaps." Maria was clearly tired of being fragmented. She wanted to be the same person with the same values on Monday at the office, on Sunday at the altar, and at home having dinner with her family. And she wasn't sure how to dismantle these divisions in her life.

But there was more. She was becoming restless with the concept of trust as *only a word*. She wanted to trust God not just in her religious practice—in an I-know-God-is-out-there way—but also in the everyday, ordinary moments of her day. And she had a genuine desire to be of service in the world.

She looked at me helplessly but there was a hint of hope in her eyes, too. And tentatively, I asked her, "Have you ever ridden a bicycle built for two?"

Though a little bewildered, she relaxed and smiled, as I shared with her my favorite imaginative essay about trust, entitled "Bicycling with God":

At first I saw God as my observer, my judge, keeping track of the things I did wrong, so as to know whether I merited heaven or hell when I die. God was out there sort of like the President. I recognized the picture, but I didn't really know God.

But later on, it seemed as though life was rather like a bike ride, but it was a tandem bike, and I noticed that God was in the back helping me pedal.

I don't know just when it was that God suggested we change places, but life has not been the same since. It's much more exciting.

When I had control, I knew the way. It was rather boring, but predictable. It was the shortest distance between two points.

But when God took the lead, God knew delightful long cuts, up mountains, and through rocky places and at breakneck speeds; it was all I could do to hang on. Even though it looked like madness, God said, "Pedal."

I worried and was anxious and asked, "Where are you taking me?" God laughed and didn't answer, but I started to trust.

I forgot my boring life and entered into the new adventure. And when I'd say, "I'm scared," God would reach back and touch my hand.

God took me to people with gifts that I needed, gifts of healing, acceptance and joy. They gave me their gifts to take on my journey . . . my journey with God.

And we were off again. God said, "Give the gifts away; they're extra baggage . . . too much weight." So I did—to the people we met. And I found that in giving I received, and still our burden was light.

I did not trust God at first, in control of my life. I thought we would wreck. But God knows "bike secrets"—how to make it bend to take sharp corners, jump to clear rocks, fly to shorten scary passages.

And I am learning to be quiet and pedal in the strangest places, and I'm beginning to enjoy the view and the cool breeze on my face with my constant companion, the Spirit of God.

And when I'm sure I just can't do any more, God just smiles and says, "Pedal." (Author Unknown)

Maria was ready to move to the "second seat," while still pedaling like crazy in her proactive way. For a while we explored what that might look like in her life. How could she move from directing to participating? How could she allow, yet act? How could she remain responsible, yet surrender to God at the same time?

She looked completely confused. "It's one thing to talk about paradox and quite another to live it," she sighed. And this dilemma belongs to all of us. We live our lives balancing many pairs of opposites—work and play, solitude and community, inner nurture and servanthood, divine sovereignty and personal free will. And it fills us with butterflies and bravery, apprehension and anticipation—more paradoxes! One plainspoken friend of mine put it candidly: "Just how do I pay the rent and take care of business, yet trust God like the proverbial lilies of the field?"

We can't do it apart from a close relationship with the spirit of God. So Maria and I began to examine the experiences that helped her feel connected to God—her traditional commitments to regular worship, prayer, Bible study, spiritual reading. Then we began to broaden that spectrum to include breath prayers, walking prayers, silence, time apart in nature—practices that connected her to her body and to creation. We talked about the ways to listen to the nuances of the "still small Voice."

Over the next few months, Maria's anxious uncertainty gave way to confidence—a blessed assurance, actually—that God would be with her no matter what unfolded. As she stopped forcing her agenda, small miracles occurred. She began to trust that God was involved in supplying her needs, like daily manna. It was time to loosen her own stranglehold on her life and allow a more integrated spirituality.

It has been wisely said that spiritual growth is marked by an increasing capacity to tolerate ambiguity and paradox. But that is far from easy for most of us. At its worst, trying to live in the tension of opposites makes us anxious; at its best, it's a creative paradox that enlivens our lives and confirms us as seekers after the truth. Religious leader and author Richard Rohr wrote of the necessity for holding this tension of the opposites in his popular book *Simplicity*:

> I've never found that a lot of wisdom comes through people who have planted themselves dogmatically somewhere or other. I have found that a great deal of wisdom comes into the world through people who creatively hold the tension of opposites on difficult and complex issues. Their outstretched arms, nailed in the truth on both sides, make them look like the crucified, who was a living icon of the opposites of human and divine, heaven and earth, male body and female soul, hanging between the good thief and the bad thief, which is the two parts of all of us. That is a magnificent image of transformation.[1]

Holding this tension between allowing God to guide us, yet being responsible partners, is like dancing, in many ways. We are essentially doing the dance of grace with God as the leading partner. Put yourself for a moment in the feminine place of dancing with a very skilled partner where every step is an automatic instinct of the body and soul, responding to the slightest nuance of the leader. The leader doesn't say, "Take one step to the right; now turn left." Rather, the familiarity and closeness of a *relationship* nurtured over time allows the following partner to *sense* the right movements.

This is an accurate metaphor, I believe, reflecting the relationship that can be ours when we allow God to lead us. We are in harmony. We are "in step." It's not a guarantee of a pain-free or problem-free life, and chances are we'll occasionally trip over our own toes and fall on our faces. But we are dancing with a Divine Partner who repeatedly picks us up, dusts us off, and invites us to continue the dance. Over time, we begin to trust this Partner with our very lives. When we begin to relax our grip on our own agenda, *we stop managing life and allow it to teach us.*

"If Only . . ."

"If only that hadn't happened to me—it wasn't in my plans." It's the recurring motif in our litany of poor choices and missed opportunities. At 3 AM on a restless night, we can be bombarded with stubborn second guesses—the "why-did-I's" and "what-if's" that plague us all—regrets that seem impossible to release. How could I have made such a mistake? Why did I say those hurtful words? Why did my parents bring me up with such baggage? If only she hadn't left me.

Our good intentions to let go and move on are easily sabotaged by renewed remorse, and a pity-party can get in high gear before we know it. Releasing regrets is one of the most daunting challenges in the letting-go process.

Nina had a checkered past that kept invading her present. She was reared in a family where anger was the chief currency of human exchange. In fact, the domestic atmosphere was so horrific that she left her Midwestern home at age eighteen, vowing never to return. But the ties couldn't be broken that easily. They wound themselves through her adult years as she began to establish her own family. She found herself in a familiar pattern of angry overreaction, lashing out indiscriminately at her children—a copycat of her parents' behavior. She had vowed not to do it, she confided to me one day, but she did it anyway.

The turbulence of her anger increased with her husband's escalating alcoholism and her sons' drug and criminal involvement. The whole family was spiraling downward. There were frightening outbursts, separations, prison sentences. And she began to reach out in desperation for a lifeline—to Al-Anon, to the church, to a counselor—but always in her private moments she maintained an ongoing conversation with God. She sat on the edge of the lake and railed at God with the candor of the Psalms of lament. She engaged her body in prayer as she literally "ran for her life." Her persistent openness allowed God to use many other instruments for her healing—therapy, nature, the lay renewal movement, the loyal support of a caring church community. Slowly, slowly, she let go of the enormous burden of guilt and shame, and peace began to replace rage. It was hard work, intentional work, repetitive work.

After more than twenty-five years, she attempted reconciliation with her three siblings and her abusive father, relating her feelings to them honestly. Confession and forgiveness flowed generously, and the family—though still somewhat fractious—took a vacation together to mark their new-found unity. It was nothing short of a miracle.

The unspoken "plan" for Nina's life had been one of continued dysfunction, living out the faulty blueprint that she inherited. By releasing the stains of the past, she opened the door to God's plan for her future. She is now the ordained minister of a mission church and is an instrument of peace and healing in the lives of the congregants.

I wonder sometimes if we're aware of the subtle sabotage we engineer by clinging to past mistakes. "If only I had done it a different way," we say remorsefully. Well, we didn't. We can't do it over. And once we've faced the truth and extracted the lessons from the situation, there comes a time where we must change our focus. We must walk away from it in order to walk forward into new life.

It isn't only in our personal lives that we invest energy in the past. We yearn repeatedly for the "good old days"; we bemoan the state of the world and the state of the church.

There is an oft-repeated maxim that goes like this: Regret of the past and fear of the future are twin thieves that rob us of the present. The effort we expend in fretting about the past and worrying about the future can suck the very life out of us, leaving little energy to focus on what is happening right in front of us. How can we stretch out our hands to receive the blessed sacrament of the present moment? We can let the past be the past. We don't live there now. Today is today, and we can place all that we are right here. In doing so, we join the ever-present power of God, as portrayed in this imaginary conversation written by Helen Mallicoat:

"My name is I Am." He paused. I waited. He continued,

—"When you live in the past, with its mistakes and regrets, it is hard. I am not there. My name is not I Was.

—When you live in the future, with its problems and fears, it is hard. I am not there. My name is not I Will Be.

—When you live in this moment, it is not hard. I am here. My name is I Am."[2]

"What If . . ."

A capable wife who can find? She is far more precious than jewels. (Prov 31:10)

What if I could have a successful, debt-free business? What if I could get tenure in my teaching job? What if I could be at the top of my profession? What if I could be . . . ? Some of our plans are difficult to let go because we never openly state them. They just sit in our consciousness like resident fixtures, underneath the articulated agendas. They are our *dreams* for ourselves. They are the content of *what we thought our lives would be.* And we usually measure our happiness against their fulfillment—or lack of it.

Once upon a time, I had a dream for my life, and the substance of it never changed. Oh, perhaps the locale, the manner of dress, and the setting varied, but not the theme. Schooled in the standards of Prov 31, describing a woman whose value was "far above rubies," I determined in some basic part of myself to be that woman. I would be treasured by my adoring husband. I would delight in my obedient children. I would reap the just rewards of a life lived "in the fear of the Lord."

I had confidence in my ability to make it happen. I would charm the man of my dreams. He would love me passionately and forever. We would have brilliant children, secure in the knowledge that they had devoted parents who would always be there for them. Each holiday would be a Currier-and-Ives clone, complete with dogs barking, the family gathering in grateful thanksgiving, and the scent of cinnamon in the air. Love and laughter would fill the house and spill over to friends. The needy would not be forgotten. The few inevitable bumps and bruises along the way would be handled bravely, and the family bond would strengthen with every passing year.

I poured all of my energies into that effort, stumbling blindly and often, living in a naïve world where "practice makes perfect" and "pretty is as pretty does." Never did I doubt that if I just kept trying hard enough, everything would be fine. But the day dawned when that idyllic world began to crumble around my feet. My husband wanted a divorce.

My rose-colored focus and fairy-tale life left me ill-prepared to deal with the ensuing feelings of rejection and loss. I was like an immigrant entering a strange land of letting go; I didn't speak the language and didn't know the customs. So very slowly, I learned to do without a husband I had idealized, a luxurious lifestyle, and—most jarring of all—my identity as a married woman. But I never let go of that dream. True happiness was linked with that ideal-woman image, stamped on my unconscious mind.

After the divorce, there were years of slow healing, when just putting one foot in front of the other felt like a victory. I found that there was a significant difference between learning to function without something or someone—surviving a loss—and truly letting go in hope. Faith in God was the rock I leaned on, and my dependence on God deepened. I began a more experiential spiritual journey, one more honest and authentic than in my years of "doing" religion. I began to explore my own inner world, eager to experience the meaning of "the Christ within." I wanted desperately to make sense out of what had happened to me.

That inner landscape was not without its deserts and demons. There were wounds to heal, guilt to confront, and failure to face. I had to wrestle with the concept of forgiveness as more than merely a repetition of the proper words. At first, I vehemently denied any anger at God, but I was fooling myself. Underneath the piety, I felt a sense of abandonment by God. I had tried my dead-level best to be a good person and had not been "blessed." Some of my Christian supporters tried to help, but their inadvertent words of judgment stung my soul. Comments such as, "Wonder what God is trying to tell you?" or "Everything happens for a reason," did little to comfort me. No matter what words were used, the feelings were those of rejection, abandonment, and punishment.

I had to *confront* that pain before I could let it go, and it took years. There were many "aha's" and "serendipities" along the way that surprised me, one in particular. I discovered that as I got to know myself better, I got to know God better. The journey to myself and the journey to God seemed to run parallel to each other. *Were self-knowledge and salvation strangely intertwined?* Slowly, a strange kind of "knowing" began to form in my soul. I finally knew—absolutely knew—in some unnamed inner space that I was unconditionally loved by God. On the one hand, my mistakes were sinful stumblings with consequences; on the other hand, they could be stepping-stones to deeper wisdom and compassion. I was going to be all right, and I knew it.

But I still didn't feel light and free and hopeful. Even with this deepening connection to God, there was still a strange heaviness of heart. Why did I continue to feel such deep sadness? Why did even my happiest moments hover over a mysterious muddiness of spirit? Why was there—underneath the joyous façade—a feeling that something was still lacking? What was this sense of "deflation" about—as if I were settling for a second-best sort of life? I knew I could survive and function, but there was no spring in my step.

The answers began to form as I prepared to lead a workshop on "The Art of Letting Go" in the summer of 1997. I had the first three sessions down pat, but the final and fourth session was flat and lifeless. I went through the lecture material I had written on the subject of letting go of people, places, things—even the need for understanding and approval. Still there was a persistent sense of incompleteness, as if some layer of awareness was yet undiscovered. I had been teaching long enough to know that I couldn't lead others to a place I hadn't been myself, so I opened myself to God for some serious soul-searching. Somewhere inside I knew my sense of confusion was somehow connected to the sadness that sat buried underneath the surface of my days, but I was reluctant to dig that deeply.

There was a clutched fist inside me that was still clinging to my dream. I still held tightly to the ideal of wife and mother as the definition of feminine success and felt that anything else was second best, an inferior way of life that one "settled" for. I hadn't let go of that plan for my life; I didn't see how I could. Yet I knew it was holding me back.

In my head, I knew I was complete without being the perfect wife and mother. After all, I reasoned, I was not called by God to be perfect; I was called to be *faithful* and to live in utter openness of spirit. But I wanted my *heart* to accept this, to soften its stubborn stance. So things hadn't worked out the way I'd planned. So what? I was tired of being weighed down with expectations. I wanted to be *free*.

But to do that, I had to allow my sadness to be transformed into something else. I had to change my life questions. "What's next?" I began asking God. "How can my mistakes be used? How can I make my life count in a new way?" *What is God's dream for me now?* As I took the first tentative steps into those threatening questions, I slowly began to live into the answers, one minute at a time. It was as if I ceased trying to do it all by myself. I allowed God to help me pick up the shattered pieces of my life and begin to construct a new mosaic—one with new colors and unexpected patterns.

My dream hasn't disappeared, nor has it ceased to be worthwhile. It is simply no longer the guiding light of my life, no longer my idol. I felt ready that day to walk into the years left to me with open hands, not with a death grip on my own agenda for happiness, clutching my limited definition of who I was and who I could become.

Thomas Keating wisely says that one of the requirements for true freedom is the dismantling of our own emotional programs. And those hidden fantasies are alive in all of us—secret dreams of the ideal spouse, the perfect job, a house in the Hamptons, sending the kids to Yale, a vocation as a potter instead of a programmer. There are family dreams, societal dreams, and even our individual versions of the American Dream. All these expectations are lodged in the unconscious and we think their fulfillment will make us happy. But somehow we must find a way to get in touch with God's dream for us. Then we can become instruments in God's dream for the world. It's a movement from fantasy to freedom.

"Whatever. . ."

> Mary said, "Here am I, the servant of the Lord; let it be with me according to your word." (Luke 1:38)

> Consider the lilies, how they grow; they neither toil nor spin; yet I tell you, even Solomon in all his glory was not clothed like one of these. But if God so clothes the grass of the field, which is alive today and tomorrow is thrown in to the oven, how much more will he clothe you—you of little faith. (Luke 12:27, 28)

"Whatever!" the apathetic teenager says with a toss of the head. We've come to associate the word with a cavalier lack of concern, an attitude of dismissal, a badge of irresponsibility. Anything goes. I don't care.

But isn't that what Mary was saying in the scriptural account in Luke 1 of the angel's visitation? When told of her selection as the Mother of Jesus, she essentially replied, "Whatever." Let it be. But it took an elderly Catholic priest to introduce this lifelong Protestant to Mary's timeless story.

We called him simply Father Ed. If his beard had been white, he would have been the perfect Santa Claus—a jolly man with an unmistakable twinkle in his eye. As a presenter at the Academy for Spiritual Formation, his week of lectures had challenged us to a posture of radical trust in God—not a casual benign intention to "be better Christians"—but the real thing. He called it abandonment, as he gave us the following prayer, penned by Brother Charles of Jesus:

> God, my Father,
> I abandon myself to you.
> Do with me what pleases you.
> Whatever you do,
> I thank you.
> I am ready for everything, I accept all,
> provided that your will
> be done in me and in all your creatures.
> I desire nothing more, my God.
> I place my soul into your hands.
> I give it to you, my God,
> with all the love of my heart,
> for I love you

and I long to give myself completely to you.
I place myself in your hands, without measure,
with infinite confidence,
for you are my Father.[3]

Some in the academy group were troubled by the choice of words, tripping on phrases like "I accept all," seeing them as a backward track for women and minorities, a kind of spiritual regression. I understood their objections, but I sensed that Father Ed meant something else entirely. He quietly and willingly received the criticism, offering no defense, but continuing to exude joy, serenity, and an enviable freedom from both criticism and approval. He said he was sorry if he offended anyone, but that "abandonment" was exactly what he posited as total commitment to Christ. All I knew was I wasn't ready to go where he was leading. Not then, anyway.

Two years later, I was ready to listen, but still tentative. My inner voice kept urging me to reconnect with this wise teacher. I heard he was speaking at a retreat center in Kentucky, so I signed up, still not sure why I was so compelled to do so. When we greeted each other, I admitted to him that I had avoided him like the plague during that academy week two years before, because I didn't want to hear what he had to say. He laughed his hearty laugh and said, "Well, you're ready when you're ready," and he invited me to meet with him that afternoon.

Father Ed introduced me to a fresh understanding of the meaning of surrender. For me, the word had always been couched in feelings of defeat, as if one were saying, "Oh, all *right*—I've tried everything else; nothing has worked, so I guess I have no choice left except to surrender to God." A faith of last resort. As I wrote earlier, surrender is not giving up. It's saying a resounding *yes*.

Father Ed also supplied a biblical foundation for his words of guidance. He suggested that I spend some significant time meditating on the story of Mary's abandonment to God as recorded in Luke 1 and allow that Scripture to speak directly to my life.

I had heard the story hundreds of times: The angel visits Mary, informs her that she, a virgin, will conceive a son, and she says, "Yes." As I re-read the story, I suddenly realized the extent to which she had to release the dream for *her* life! Certainly, as a young woman of thirteen or fourteen, it wouldn't have been her plan to become pregnant out of wedlock in a society that might shun or harm her, to live a life of uncertainty and sadness, and to have her son cruelly killed.

I doubt she planned to give birth to her first child in a smelly, unsanitary stable with barn animals as helpless onlookers. I'll bet in reality it was a far from happy evening, hardly like the sterilized and romanticized version that we sing about at Christmas. Mary was probably cold, hungry, scared, and in pain. But somehow, she *let it be*. Knowing nothing of what lay ahead of her, she said, "Let it be with me according to your word." In some small way, we follow in her faithful footsteps when we let go of the dream of our lives and trust God's dream.

At first, it was frightening to think that surrendering to God might open me to even more heartache. I'd always equated letting go with hardship and sacrifice. But surprisingly, this relinquishment didn't *feel* like defeat; it felt hopeful, passionate, *free*. It seems a shame that the directive to "follow your bliss" has received such bad press in some religious circles. Many have come to associate it with new-age self-indulgence and navel-gazing narcissism. The truth is there is deep joy in connecting with the soul's authenticity—a kind of bliss that's independent of circumstances. Surely the Creator God engineered our complex systems of mind, body, and spirit with such beautiful interconnectedness that we can pay attention to the resonance we experience when we're true to ourselves—a peace that passes all understanding. But to experience it, we must loosen our tight grip on our plans.

What would happen if we made "whatever" a code word for surrender? Suppose we dropped all resistance to life. Suppose we flowed with it, one little step at a time, without attempting to control the outcome. Doing those things aren't signs of weakness, but of strength. Spiritual surrender also requires paying attention to opportunities and *taking action on what we know so far*. If we believe that part of God's will for us is that we become *whole*, then we must *allow* that wholeness and well-being—not try to make it happen.

This need to control—to plan and implement outcomes—is our cultural bias. We grow up with the illusion that we are, and can be, and *should be* in control of our lives. This idol requires that we devote our time and energy, our hearts and souls, to keeping this illusion alive—and we do. Often we don't recognize our compulsion to control because it's cloaked with good intentions and justified by worthwhile goals. We seek to control others to get them to "do the right thing"; we seek to control the spirit of God through our prayers; we want our country to be in control of world affairs, no matter how many bombs we have to drop to accomplish that. Many of us are terrified of losing control of our lives through sickness. Dying looms as the final challenge to our control; we see death as an enemy to be defeated.

In fact, the ability to plan and control the outcome of events is so revered—and ingrained in us—that it can contaminate even our best motives.

For example, when my sons were grammar-school age, I thought it was my job as a good parent to manage their lives, to *control* their development rather than to allow it. I wanted them to develop a heart of compassion, so—with my usual proactive posture—I set out to make that happen. One year during our annual church Christmas Basket project, I got the name of a local family in need and determined to involve the children. We secured the names and ages of the family's children, and I took the boys on shopping trips to select toys and clothes. We wrapped the gifts in festive paper, purchased mountains of groceries, a huge turkey, and loaded the station wagon to the gills with all the bounty. Then we headed off to the housing project on the other side of town with hearts full of a holiday spirit of generosity and sharing. It was a kind of controlled experiment in Christian charity—or so I thought.

When we arrived at the shabby apartment late in the day, my timid knock at the door was answered by a disheveled woman, who looked at me suspiciously through a crack in the door. I eagerly told her why we had come and with obvious reluctance she let us into her home. Cheerfully, we introduced ourselves to the children and unloaded all the packages and parcels of food. Almost immediately she mumbled a hasty thank-you and hastened us out the door. Hardly the sort of gratitude I expected.

As we were leaving the porch, we encountered another unexpected surprise. "Hey, you!" a man shouted from next door. "Didn't you bring me anything? I need some Christmas too, ya know!" Taken aback and frightened by his anger, we hurried to the car and drove back to our safe little neighborhood. My expectations of an object lesson in the joy of giving were down the drain. So much for controlling my children's formation in Christian compassion.

But the greater lesson was yet to be learned, not by the children, but by me. The incident wouldn't fade from my mind. As the days passed, and my righteous anger finally turned to prayerful consideration, I finally realized my hubris. I hadn't even given a thought to the embarrassment the woman must have felt in seeing strangers give her children the Christmas *she* wanted to give them herself. I hadn't considered the shame she may have experienced in being a charity case. I was overcome with remorse. For a moment, I forgot the separation between us and my heart was able to feel her despair. *We were both mothers.* Not only did I feel her shame; I felt my shame, too.

I had to admit to myself that the act of mercy had been just as much about my needs as hers. Or her angry neighbor's. The protesting man outside the door was no doubt frustrated by the sight of piles of provisions when he, too, was in need. That incident occurred more than thirty years ago, and I can still feel the sting of sadness at my own callousness. My effort to control a "lesson" for my own children had blinded me to the true nature of another's pain.

Much of our manipulative behavior is so unconscious and automatic that we don't even recognize it. In fact, we often label *others* as control freaks, not ourselves. When we want someone to do or think something, we seek to engineer the outcome we want, rather than assuming the open posture of "whatever." This is understandably a thorny issue for parents. We feel the responsibility to steer our children toward worthwhile plans and purposes; at the same time, we understand the need to let them pursue their own goals.

There are parents, for instance, who push their children unmercifully "for their own good." I knew a young man whose youth was sacrificed in pursuit of excellence on the tennis court. Daily lessons consumed the after-school time slot. Other parts of his life were put on hold, unexplored, undeveloped, unlived. Yes, he received the tennis scholarship that his parents had insisted was his ticket to college. But the cost was high. His growing resentment erupted in an abandonment of his college career, the covering of his body with defiant tattoos, and the acceptance of the label—*failure*. He ended up despising the sport that had consumed his youth. His breach with his parents is still not reconciled.

Breadwinners sometimes attempt to control other family members through financial means. They often commandeer the parents' Golden Rule in an effort to lace the underlying truth with humor, "The one with the gold makes the rules." And this is not only the domain of domineering fathers. I watched a doting mother send her daughter away to college, but not away from her control. She continued to cling to her daughter and sustain their relationship through dollars and dependency. It didn't work.

Certainly, there is a place for persuasion, for trying to influence the actions of another. But it should be open and above-board—not used as leverage for love. Nor should it be punctuated with guilt-producing statements like, "After all I've sacrificed for you," or "I work hard all day long, and look at the thanks I get," or "I'm paying all this money so that you can have a life better than I had." Though the statements may have some truth in them, their manipulative nature dooms them to defeat.

Perhaps the most common and insidious form of attempted control, especially by women, is manipulation through guilt. We seek to manage others by subtle statements indicating how much their actions or opinions affect our well-being. If we make them feel guilty enough, we unconsciously reason, then they'll do what we think they should. Tears, whining, and nagging are tools of the trade, though they're often cloaked in pious terms.

The truth is that all our efforts to "say this so they'll think that" or "do this and they'll do that" are far from a sure thing. We must come to grips with the absolute truth that control is an illusion. *We may have influence, but not control.* Our freedom comes through doing what we think is appropriate, valid, and loving, then *letting go of the outcome*. In fact, it's a good idea to incorporate an internal checklist to help us interrupt our knee-jerk control behaviors:

- Is it appropriate?
- Is it valid?
- Is it honest?
- Is it loving?

Oddly enough, when we relinquish our attempts to control, a strange serendipity sometimes occurs. Some sort of inner dynamic is freed up, and the situation changes with no effort or input on our part. But in any case, freedom is the outcome.

What about the other side of the coin? What do we do when others try to control *us*? To be clear, others can't control us without our permission. It takes two to play that game. As we become more aware of our own tendencies to control, we begin to identify the same tactics on the part of others. It becomes our responsibility to set appropriate boundaries—a lifelong project for many of us who are accustomed to allowing ourselves to be manipulated in the name of love.

Agnes was constantly being manipulated by her children. Her adult son loved her dearly but had a habit of using her that was probably unconscious to both of them. When he needed money or other favors, he engaged her in meaningful conversation, which cemented the warm bond that they shared. After a time, when Agnes had relaxed into their pleasant exchange, he would segue into his request, "By the way, Mom, I'm really in a jam . . ." When his promises to repay her were consistently broken, she reluctantly set firm boundaries, denying him any more loans. In the short term, their relationship was rocky, but ultimately her actions contributed to the financial independence he needed to develop. The penchant for control is alive in others as well as in us.

As we summon the awareness and the courage to release control of our own lives, sacred space is created for the growth of genuine trust. Trust that there is a benevolent order to the world. Trust that the Spirit of God *cares*. And with more trust comes less resistance to life. And we stand ready to accept "whatever. . . ," knowing that God walks into the unknown with us.

"I Surrender"

> Those who find their life will lose it, and those who lose their life for my sake will find it. (Matt 10:39)

> But if you forget about yourself and look to me, you'll find both yourself and me. (Matt 10:39)[4]

> But seek first his kingdom, and all these things shall be yours as well. (Matt 6:33)

All letting go is essentially about death—the death of bondage and the birth of freedom. The tiny little ego-deaths that make room for love and compassion. That truth is lived out for all of us on multiple levels, including the ultimate letting go that we share—that of our own lives.

"You have such *potential*," she was told repeatedly during her growing-up years. Bright, competent, popular, Susan had the world by the tail. She had even fulfilled her vocational dream of graduating from law school in her late thirties. And then one of her eyes began to behave in a peculiar fashion. It seemed to be little more than a distracting intrusion in her vision, but it wouldn't go away.

Preliminary tests were taken, and she could tell from the look on the doctor's face that the news wasn't good. Further tests revealed that she had a rare melanoma of the eye. After the initial shock, she underwent the recommended procedures, spent a week in the hospital surrounded by friends and family, and the tumor seemed to have vanished.

But a year later, the systemic condition showed up in her liver. This time the prognosis was more guarded and grim, and she began to accept the fact that her days might be numbered, perhaps to as little as one year. In an instant, all the pieces of her life were thrown up in the air. Her values were shuffled like a deck of cards.

Her customary knee-jerk reaction to "make others proud of her" had still been the driving force. She was courageous, positive, eager to maintain control of her life. But this second appearance of the cancer, accompanied by more serious surgery, began to shatter her illusion of control. As she slowly let go of her need to meet others' expectations, she realized that the expectations were *her own*, not those of family and friends. They loved her unconditionally for *herself*. They merely wanted her to *be*.

Letting go of these expectations, both external and internal, paved the way for genuine feelings of hope and acceptance. As she relinquished her status as "the big planner," she noticed some interesting changes—delightful serendipities. The burdens of the past—regrets, guilt—didn't carry the weight they had before. Even anxiety about her future began to melt away in the growing trust. She was left with an exhilarating focus on the present, an intense treasuring of her relationships. She found that she didn't want to merely *save* her life; she wanted to *savor* it.

Susan began to understand the profound difference between expectation and hope. Expectation is attached to agenda, removing surprise and thwarting possibility. Hope reflects inner wholeness; hope is open-ended and full of possibility.

Even her relationship with God underwent transformation. God as Distant Deity became God as Loving Friend. There was a growing sense of companionship, acceptance, divine support—the "blessed assurance" that she had sung about all her life.

All of us share this ultimate letting go of our lives. And somehow, serious illness provides a sort of "dress rehearsal" that boils life down to its essence, to the components that really matter. Tragedies of every kind have a way of distilling our values. There's no room for resentment and regrets, for grumbling and griping. Other concerns rise to the top, dominated by questions like, "How well have I loved? Is what I think, do, stand for, and speak in the service of love?" Surrendering our lives to God is not a matter of sitting back in defeated resignation. Rather, we lean forward into a greater Love that can fill us and flow through us. We *join in* the creative work of God.

Gerald May wrote in *Will and Spirit* that "true spiritual surrender is conscious, intentional, and responsible; one accepts the consequences. Without fanfare, without pretense to heroism, one simply chooses to take a step." He explains further that "spiritual surrender engages mystery. It opens itself to the unknown."[5]

Even deeper than the release of our physical lives is the surrender of the ego's life. The perplexing Scripture, "He who loses his life shall find it" may not be so much a command of God as a statement of how human life works. Karen Armstrong, in her stirring autobiography, *The Spiral Staircase*, muses about this human condition: "If you cast your bread upon the waters and were prepared to give it up for good, it would somehow come back to us—albeit in another form."[6]

In some ways, spiritual growth is about a series of what are called "ego-deaths." But there's a paradox here. It seems to me that the ego doesn't disappear so much as it is no longer in charge, in the driver's seat, on the front of the bike. In fact, one must have a well-defined ego before one can choose to let it go. Much of the work of the spiritual journey is learning to recognize this unconscious dominance of the ego in all that we do—our subtle manipulations, our persistent self-interest.

If we pay close attention, we can tell when the ego is in charge. Some sure signs are: a tendency toward hurt feelings, persistent irritability, a need for self-defense, a penchant for pleasing others, feelings of competition, a desire to be thanked or recognized. Often we see these qualities in others, but fail to detect them in ourselves, so great is our capacity for self-deception.

Relinquishing the ego paves the way for this "finding of our lives" that the Scriptures speak of, the "true Self" in psychological terms. In any language, it means that we find out who we truly are. Rather than lose our personality in a sea of spiritual blandness, God enlivens us to be true to ourselves, to see our own unique identity in neon letters ten feet tall. Remember, we don't totally banish the ego; we voluntarily place it in the service of the higher Self, which is united in God.

PRAYER

God of many names,
My name is known to you.
I am held in the hand of your life,
And I do not know what you will make of me.
All I know is that I cannot make myself
Anymore than I could in my mother's womb.
But this I can do,
This I choose,
To give myself into the hand of your continuing creativity.
My past, with its joys and triumphs, its failures and regrets.
My present, with its struggles and accomplishments, its hopes and setbacks.
My future, with its fears and freedom, its pain and promise.
To loose and to bind, to stretch and to shape,
To become what I will.
Trusting the hand that made the world,
Trusting the spirit that breathes life,
Trusting the love that will not let me go,
Trusting the promise of the Word made flesh. Amen.

Kathy Galloway[7]

For Reflection

1. Are there events or people in your past to which you are still clinging? Is it time to let them go?

2. How do you react when there's a change in plans? When you don't get what you want? What internal movement might help you to be more accepting and flexible?

3. What was your dream for your life? Does it need to be modified or let go?

4. What is the primary barrier that keeps you from a sincere surrender to God's will in your life?

Part III
Letting Go—How?

Ask, and it will be given to you; seek, and you will find; knock, and the door will be opened for you. (Matt 7:7)

Let one who seeks continue seeking until he finds. When he finds, he will be troubled. When he is troubled, he will be astonished.

—Lost Gospel of Thomas[1]

The top was down on the red Mercedes convertible, and smiling in the front passenger seat—*my* seat—was the petite beauty with the flowing blonde ponytail, seated happily beside my ex-husband. I swallowed hard, glued a plastic grin on my face, and ushered my handsome sons, ten and fifteen, out the door. I caught a glimpse of their confused faces—reflecting their painful inner conflict. "I'm so glad to see Dad" was doing battle with "How can I leave Mom all alone?" I stood on the threshold that Sunday afternoon, waving and smiling, hearing myself say, "Have a good time, boys!"

As they drove away, I crumpled to the floor in a heap—like a pile of bones wrapped around a heart that barely remembered how to beat. How much longer could I pull off this phony act? How could I continue to pretend this was *normal*? Part of me knew that, try as I might, I was in too much agony to see the situation clearly. I had to have help—*real* help, not sympathy.

So I called Dr. Walton Harrison. He was our across-the-alley neighbor, a wise pediatrician who had worked with kids for more than forty years. He had offered his assistance right after the divorce three months earlier, but I hadn't taken him up on it then. I had been too much in shock to even formulate a question for him. Since our family didn't know Dr. Harrison very well, I felt there would be a healthy professional distance. So, in a matter of minutes, I was seated in the Harrisons' living room with a cup of coffee, spilling my guts.

"I feel so *phony*," I complained. "I send the boys off in the car with their father and his fiancée, as if I *approved* of it, as if it's okay with me! It's a lie; I'm dying inside when I see them drive away. How can I behave so dishonestly with my children?" I went on to describe the feelings of rage and betrayal, as well as the well-intentioned advice of friends that I shouldn't allow the boys to go out with the new couple. I told him I didn't know what to do.

Dr. Harrison listened quietly to my ranting, then said very gently, "Linda, are you asking me what is best for your two sons in this situation?" When I nodded yes, he added profoundly, "Take a deep breath. You're not going to like what I have to say; it's going to hurt."

He was right. He explained the inner conflict that a divorce creates in the psyches of children as they try to figure out how to please both parents, how to *love* both parents. He described their frantic attempts to make everything okay, to find a way to hold on to one parent without hurting the other. Then he added, "I'm not asking you to ignore your pain. On the contrary. Get your feelings out with your friends; come over here to our house if you like. Rant and rage as much as you need to—*but not in front of your children*. It will create an internal struggle that can cripple them for years to come."

I sat in stunned silence, trying to absorb this troubling truth. I hadn't yet thought about the long-lasting implications of divorce on the lives of innocent children. And, thankfully, an overwhelming need to protect my sons gave me strength to listen to the rest of it.

"Try not to say one single derogatory word about their father or about his fiancée—ever," he stated clearly. "The healthiest outcome of this situation is for the children to be absolutely loved and accepted in *both* homes."

I felt as if the air had been knocked out of me. It didn't seem fair, I protested. I was being asked to do the impossible! His advice went against everything I was feeling inside and everything I was hearing outside.

And he wasn't finished. "That means not asking for a 'report' of their evening with their father—no questions about what he said, or she said. No thinly disguised probing to goad the children into evaluating the new woman in their father's life or to influence their feelings in a negative way."

As I wept and confessed that I didn't know if I could do it, he said gently, "I know. This will be very, very hard. And you won't be able to do it one hundred per cent of the time. Just do it as consistently as you can, and be ready to forgive yourself for the inevitable times when your resentment gets the best of you."

We went on to discuss particular ways to make the visits easier for everyone. To my surprise, he suggested that I plan some specific outing for *myself* to coincide with the absence of the boys—a movie, dinner with friends—something that might alleviate their guilt at leaving Mom alone.

Dr. Harrison was right about that one, too. When the next visit rolled around, I said cheerfully, "As soon as you leave, fellas, I'm headed to the movie with some buddies. I'll leave the key under the mat in case you get back before I do." The relief on their faces was the only encouragement I needed.

I don't want to make this sound easier or neater than it was. There were many tough situations during the months and years that followed—school programs, birthdays, graduations, eventually the boys' weddings—all occasions when the two families needed to unite to support David and Harrison. But Dr. Harrison's advice to act consistently out of my highest instincts was a guiding light to me, even when it came across to others as idealistic naivete. I'm still convinced that taking the high road made for a much smoother ride.

I still struggle to explain what actually happened that day in Dr. Harrison's living room, how his direct, no-nonsense wisdom had such an impact on my life. To begin with, there was a deep sense of rightness—an inner resonance—that I recognized in his words. Somehow, his offering of safety and acceptance to *me* made it possible for me to provide safety and acceptance for my children. Even though I knew I was a long way from being able to implement his advice, he gave me the courage to take just the next step in bypassing my vindictive feelings.

In response to my plea of "Tell me what to do," he offered me behavioral tools to help me act responsibly as I entered the long process of accepting a situation I could not change. Without commiserating or judging, he accepted the difficulty of the situation and re-directed my focus from the past to the *present*.

Contained within that story is a rough microcosm of the letting-go process itself, a kind of framework for looking objectively at what happens, whether one is letting go of a person, a persona, a perspective, a pattern, or a plan. The spiritual movement seems to naturally divide itself into five basic parts, each flowing into the other, back and forth, without defined boundaries.

First, you become *aware* that something has to change.

Second, you make yourself *available* to new wisdom.

Third, you *act* responsibly on the insights you receive.

Fourth, you *allow* the healing process to begin.

Fifth, you *accept* the realities of life as they are.

Life offers many tools that can pave the way through these vital stages—from prayer to play, from counseling to creativity, from inner work to outer work—a virtual buffet of choices. You don't have to eat them all. Experiment with the exercises and suggestions—chew on them—and follow the ones that seem to suit your unique palate. Some of these spiritual "foods" will facilitate your letting-go process more than others. Take a bite here and there, and see what satisfies your hunger.

Awareness

When the Spirit of Truth comes, he will guide you into all the truth. . . (John 16:13)

. . . listening with what St. Benedict calls "the ear of the heart." The ear of the heart hears the voice of God above the voices of the world. It hears the voice of hope in the midst of despair, the voice of calm in the midst of fear, the voice of new life in the midst of death. —The Rev. Mimsy Jones[1]

Sometimes we have no idea what we're holding onto or why. Sometimes we're afraid to find out. Sometimes we'd prefer to just leave things as they are, even though our soul is nudging us out of our complacency. Though we have a tendency to cling to the familiar, we find our deepest growth in what I call "the taffy pull"—that is, the spiritual push and pull that usually yields something very sweet.

There are some barriers to growth that are easy to spot—traits or habits that we can immediately identify. But what about the ones that are hidden in the unconscious? What about the motivating forces that direct our decisions without our conscious knowledge? How do we discover the names of those powerful forces? Remember, we can't let go of something we don't even know we're clutching. We must know ourselves intimately and honestly—both the good and the bad—and tell the truth to ourselves. Befriending our shadow stuff—the stuff often hidden in our unconscious—opens the door to transforming it.

As serious seekers have shared their struggles with me in spiritual guidance sessions, I have noticed the practices that time and time again seem to bring people to awareness, help them face the nitty-gritty of where they're stuck, wake them up to *what is*. Here are some avenues to that awareness.

Prayer

> Be still and know that I am God. (Ps 46:10)

The spiritual life is sometimes pictured as a large house with many windows, surrounded by Light. It may be dark inside, but we manage to function. However, if we'll just open a window, the Light will pour in and illuminate everything in the house.

Those windows are the spiritual disciplines or tools through which we open ourselves to the Light of God—tools like worship, prayer, Scripture, journaling, simplicity, service—all ways of allowing God to work with us. No matter which window we open, the Light comes in. We can crack one window and welcome a little Light; we can throw many of them open wide, and Light can pour in. We can choose which windows we open and when. These "windows to God," the spiritual disciplines, are not holy in themselves. The purpose of any tool is to move us beyond the discipline itself to the experience of God's Light.

One of my childhood memories is that of piling the whole family into the car and going house-hunting on Sunday afternoons. House-wishing was more like it. Daddy was a postal worker and Mother was a stay-at-home mom, so for economic reasons, there was lots of dreaming. In those days, they had a fascination for "picture windows"—huge, unpaned glass expanses on the front of the fifties ranch-style houses that allowed sunlight to flood the living room. When it comes to increasing our awareness, the "picture window" is the practice of prayer.

Not just any kind of prayer, but the silent, contemplative prayer that I mentioned in chapter 7. Most people give prayer a functioning meaning, defining it as a well-intentioned effort to get something—health, peace of mind, good fortune. To be sure, petitionary prayer has its place, but—make no mistake about it—it's a type of prayer that we can *control*. We decide for whom to pray; we decide which verse to project for meditation; in other words, we handle the agenda.

In contemplative prayer, we open ourselves to a healing, transforming energy that we can't predict, direct, or control. We choose trust—*radical* trust. The contemplative mind doesn't need to judge or decide, but offers the heart and soul to God as is. We open ourselves to the Mystery, trusting in a God that is more wise and loving than we can fathom. We remove our linear measuring sticks and dissolve any expectations. In other words, we don't sit in silence for twenty minutes, then search for results with our usual way of evaluating. And that's a tough assignment for most of us production-oriented folks.

Why is this nonjudgmental stance so difficult for us? I remember the frustration of trying to measure some "spiritual progress" when I was awkwardly beginning a silent practice. I automatically wanted to quantify the experience, have some evidence that something was happening. After a period of floundering in exasperation, I finally realized I was applying this world's success model to the realm of the spirit. It just wouldn't fit. I needed to stop evaluating and simply believe the witness of centuries of prayer masters, who urge us to just show up and keep our rendezvous with God. Period. We don't have to make it happen. True contemplation is a gift.

All I can honestly say is that, over time, something *did* happen. I began to notice seemingly minor epiphanies—almost undetectable changes in both awareness and reactions. I noticed my tendency to automatically judge and categorize others, even as I was promoting tolerance in every opinion I expressed. I became aware of my subtle attempts to manipulate. Little a-ha's would bubble up unbidden, usually not at prayer time, but days or weeks later in the midst of some unrelated circumstance.

This gentle light of awareness didn't accuse me. It seemed like a silent whisper deep in my heart that was more an invitation than a command, an awareness that communicated, "There's something you might want to look at now." At first I was naïve and arrogant enough to think there was a finite list of issues that I could "work through" and conquer. What a joke. Now I know that the layers of my disharmony with the divine are endless, and that I will be shown the next layer to be peeled back, then the next and the next and the next. This growth of awareness becomes a way of life. What once was *fear* of discovering the next dysfunction became an *anticipation* of the next lesson the Spirit would teach me. Along the way, I've found that—difficult though it may be—the quieter I am, the more I will hear. Silence is truly the training ground for the art of listening. In fact, did you realize that "listen" is an anagram of "silent"?

Not only do the mystics refer to silence as "the language of God," but also as the *frequency*—the very vibration or wavelength—of God. Let me explain. If I want to tune in to classical music in Memphis, I turn my radio dial to 91.1, the frequency that puts me in touch with that kind of music. Silence is the "frequency" of God, which tunes our hearts to God's transforming presence. In the words of the old gospel hymn, "Come, Thou fount of every blessing; *tune* my heart to sing Thy grace."

John 15 teaches us, "God is Spirit, and those who worship God worship in spirit and in truth." There's obviously a reference here to unspoken communication, wordless union. This kind of silent prayer is not a matter of closing our lips and allowing the mind to continue the chatter. Remember, this is not the silence of a graveyard, but the silence of a *garden growing*. It involves the kind of emptying that tills the soil of the soul, readying it for the divine planting of seeds—seeds that will ultimately yield the fruits of the spirit in unexpected ways.

Will you experience an onslaught of thoughts? Absolutely. Will it seem impossible to control your wandering mind? To be sure. As we still the mind, voices inside our heads compete for our attention, like hummingbirds on a holiday. But eventually the forces become friendlier.

Though there are many avenues to contemplation, I'm most familiar with the practice of centering prayer, which seems particularly well suited to the

process of letting go. This method resembles the practice of calisthenics—
spiritual calisthenics. It exercises the "muscle" of letting go so consistently that
the movement of release seeps into our external life without our direction. It
establishes a kind of spiritual "muscle memory." Though centering prayer is
sometimes mistakenly viewed as something that removes us from the real
world, the truth is that it brings us more deeply *into* life. It blurs the divisions
between sacred and secular. In a miraculous way, it *integrates* us.

The practice is simple, but not easy:

1. Choose a sacred word as the symbol of your intention to consent to
   God's presence and action within.

2. Sitting comfortably and with eyes closed, settle briefly and silently
   introduce the sacred word.

3. When you become aware of thoughts, let them go, returning ever so
   gently to the sacred word.

4. At the end of the prayer period (twenty minutes is suggested), remain
   in silence with eyes closed for a couple of minutes.

It helps to read a good manual defining the process and to engage the support of others, but neither is essential. Besides Keating's book, *Open Mind,
Open Heart,* one of the finest guides to centering prayer is *Centering Prayer and
Inner Awakening* by Cynthia Bourgeault.[2] This practice has enriched the lives
of so many seekers that there are groups all over the country devoted to this
prayer method.

The writings and ministry of Flora Slosson Wuellner have also provided
a healing balm for many. In her books *Prayer and Our Bodies* and *Heart of
Healing, Heart of Light,* she composes step-by-step instructions for meditations designed to help the reader let go of wounds, of anger, even of worry
about the problems of loved ones. Many prayers include Scripture verses to
help focus the mind, then deepen into a series of images. The following sample of her imaginative style could be especially useful when worries are con-
suming us.

> Think of someone you're worried about. Relax, breathing, asking that
> the eyes of your heart open. Begin to see or sense the hurt, the unhealed
> wound, or the heavy burden within this person. Picture God's hands
> closing gently around the wounded heart of the other, the way your
> hand would close around a small, frightened bird, warming and calming
> it. Hold this image as long as seems right. Then sense the radiant light
> within this person, picturing the power of God awakening and releasing
> happiness and giftedness within. Afterward, lay your hands on your own
> heart, identifying the wound of worry there. Sense God's hands very
> gently cradling your agitated heart, holding it also like a frightened
> wounded bird.[3]

Many types of contemplative and meditative prayer practices serve to give God an opportunity to break into our limited awareness, releasing the identity of our barriers. Somehow when we stop speaking, the Divine Presence speaks.

Journaling

In the words of author Jan Johnson, "Within the rhythm of our relationship with God, there are times when prayer and meditation seem too ethereal; but the concrete act of gripping a pen seems just right."[4] Journaling from the heart is another potential pathway to awareness.

Remember the compact five-year diaries of our youth, those we kept under lock and key? They may have begun as daily news reports of teenage comings and goings, but deeper thoughts would always sneak between the lines. Spiritual journaling, too, moves beyond the mere description of life events. Rather, it provides a space to see the pattern our lives are weaving. If a journal answers just one question, it is this: What is God doing in my life?

To prime the pump of heightened awareness, we need to allow the yearnings of our hearts to travel straight down the arm to the pen and onto the page without going through the head. That ever-present mental editor needs to be sent packing! No need to pay attention to spelling, punctuation, speed, writing style, grammar—just clean out the corners of consciousness—the trash as well as the treasures. Somehow journaling provides legible proof that we want to walk and talk with God.

Day after day, it's there for God to see (our only audience) and for us to see—scattered thoughts, unthinkable questions, heretical doubts, embarrassing confessions. As we write, we can ask God to reorganize all our disorder into peace and purpose. And in that quiet discipline, we develop an ongoing conversation with God.

Some of the psalms of David seem to have functioned as his journal.

He states what happens: "I pursued my enemies . . ." (Ps 18:37)

He records his feelings: "When I am afraid . . ." (Ps 56:3)

He is candid with God about what he wants: "Deliver me . . ." (Ps 6:4)

David's hard honesty reveals that journaling is a place to be our true selves and to offer our real (though often unflattering and misguided) views of life. We can pour out our anguish, make outlandish statements—and in so doing we can stumble across our true motives, feelings, and desires. In a journal, we find the freedom to meander back to God at our own pace. Like David, we can move from hopelessness to praise, from doubt to devotion—sometimes all on the same page—wherever the spirit leads us in our growing awareness.

Clarice had always considered herself a journaler with a jinx. Though an avid reader and lover of words, she told me one day, "I've tried to journal and have failed repeatedly. I just sit there with a pen in my hand and have no idea what to write. I guess it's something I don't have a talent for." But spiritual journaling is not about writing ability—it's about availability. You begin by letting go of all rules and regulations and put down your jumbled thoughts and phrases in a random, but persistent, way. Eventually, as you get out of the driver's seat, your mind relaxes and quits composing. You let the soul breathe, *give it a voice*, and begin listening. Fresh insights will yield a heightened awareness as God speaks through the voice of your own soul.

Though we've been taught in school to figure out what we think before writing it, the opposite method works better in spiritual journaling. We figure out what we think by first writing it. Writing about our confusion invites God to enter the chaos and move us toward clarity. We slowly begin to see with the eyes of God.

Writer Madeleine L'Engle calls journaling her "free psychiatrist's couch" where she dumps all her emotional garbage and frustrations. Often in so doing, she can see her way of participating in stormy situations and becomes aware of her next step of growth. Sometimes, miraculously, the insights she needs appear right on the page in front of her.

Journaling doesn't answer all our unanswered questions. At times, it becomes the reservoir of our questions. What am I holding on to? Why am I trying to control this? How can I let it go? This keeps us in a listening mode, open and watching for God's answers to surprise us in the course of our days.

I challenge you to try this discipline daily for a month. Buy yourself a blank book with an inviting, provocative cover. Keep the writing private, simple, and free of judgment. I think you will hear the voice of God whispering through the pages.

Dreams

> I will praise the Lord, who counsels me; even at night my heart instructs me. (Ps 16:7, NIV)

I used to think that dreams were just neurons firing in the head—the flotsam and jetsam of the brain's overcrowding. Not any more. When I learned a bit about dream language and experienced some dreams that clearly pointed the way down my path to wholeness, I began to take them more seriously.

Certainly, the biblical writers did. Consider the respected status of dreams in both the Old and New Testaments—all the way from the vivid dreams of the Joseph story in Genesis to the spectacular symbolism of the Revelation to John on the island of Patmos. Many groups today are reclaiming this ancient tradition of paying attention to dream content, some even referring to them as "personal letters from God."

Some schools of thought assert that dreams are unconscious material seeking to be made conscious. The dream always belongs to the dreamer and any suggestions about the meaning of the symbols must resonate with the dreamer. Dreams are multi-layered and are usually subject to several valid interpretations. I've found that it's almost impossible to discover the golden nugget in my own dreams through my own efforts. It's more productive to work with a trained individual or in a group setting where the participants have studied reliable texts on the subject. Dream study groups are springing up all over the country; some are outgrowths of book studies of *Natural Spirituality* by Joyce Hudson.[5]

Most of us think our dreams are just too bizarre to have any significance, much less to serve as a valid vehicle for our journey to wholeness. But the craziest dreams can often yield the most fruit. Even those that seem nightmarish can contain very positive, encouraging information, when viewed by those who are familiar with symbolic dream language. For instance, I once heard renowned dream leader Robert Johnson say that dreams "have no manners." The symbols through which they communicate are graphic, earthy, natural— and occasionally embarrassing.

As I hear the dreams of those I accompany in spiritual direction, as well as those presented in a local dream group, I'm continually amazed at the wealth of information that can be gleaned.

Here are a few examples of dreams shared by those in a local dream group:

I enter a classroom with a guide beside me, who says, "This party really got out of hand!" There are bloody, dismembered limbs and body parts of the children and teachers scattered everywhere. However, each dismembered head has a faint smile on it. We are aghast, but strangely calm. I tell the guide unemotionally that I'm glad my children are in another classroom. We step carefully through the carnage, and the guide says, "I'll show you a better way." We leave the room and enter a long hall, simple and uncluttered, with clean, blank walls on each side. I can't see the end of it, but it dissolves into pure light.

The dreamer's association of the scene was with the school her children attended when they were young. Her counselor wisely asked her, "What was your life like then?" The reply brought her to tears. "I was trying to be everything to everybody—a good wife, a good mother, a leader at church, a caretaker for aging parents, a community leader." Obviously, she was remembering a period of intense fragmentation, where she felt emotionally torn apart. She always kept a smile on her face no matter what chaos reigned inside her. She rarely displayed emotion. The dream was inviting her to simplify her life, establish clear boundaries, and move toward the Light. She was being encouraged to let go of her effort to meet everyone's needs but her own.

I am in a weaving class setting. I don't have the yarns I need and must go back home to get some, where many people are bustling about. I can't find the exact thickness of yarns I think should be used for the project. I consider just taking the table loom with Navajo weaving already started, but I decide that it isn't appropriate for the project. I am side-tracked and distracted by the chaos. I can't seem to get it together, even changing blouses or sweaters several times. I finally put on my favorite outfit and leave the old weaving at home. I am eager to return to class and get started weaving a new fabric.

Through personal associations and reflections, guided by questions from her counselor, the dreamer had some startling realizations. Newly retired, she felt the weaving theme referred to her attempt to "weave" her life together in a new way. Her home life was out of kilter as she tried to establish new priorities and find the right "pieces" (yarns) for her new "project" (life). In her waking life, she was fascinated by earth-centered theology and philosophy and felt in tune with it. But it seemed that the dream was telling her this was not exactly suited to her; it was just one of the "yarns." So she was continuing to sample ways of being, changing the appearance (clothes) of her life. The dream was urging her to put on what was natural and pleasing to her, to bring creativity to her future.

I am in a two-story house where the family lives in private quarters upstairs. I go downstairs to host a church gathering. I am soon bored with the whole event and feel boxed in. Someone makes a snide comment, which I turn into a clever, sexy retort, which is very funny. Everyone gasps in righteous disapproval. I feel fed up and launch into an angry defense, shouting, "This who I am!" I then order the guests to leave my house. As they depart, some of the younger attendees leave identically wrapped gifts for me on the dining room sideboard. I go upstairs to tell my family what I have done and make no apologies about it. My family doesn't protest, but tells me lovingly that my behavior was a bit "over the top." I feel somewhat giddy and empowered.

This dreamer realizes it is time to let go of her buried resentments against the constrictive atmosphere of her upbringing as a preacher's kid and have the courage to be totally herself. Those who value her authenticity leave her gifts of affirmation. All guilt is released, and her family supports her movement toward wholeness.

I am at a party where a video is being shown. In the film, my husband and I are playing tennis—in top form. There are happy scenes with our children from years ago. The memories are so warm and poignant that I begin to cry. Two friends from that same time period in our lives come late to the party bringing caramel cake, but I tell them it's too late to serve it. I try to show the video again, this time in another room on a screenless radio. Of course, it's impossible; it doesn't work.

For this woman, this dream held many symbols of an earlier era—tennis, young children, young friends, even a radio. She grieves the loss of this sweet and tender time in her life, but it can't be replayed. It's too late. Time to let go of the past and move on to another stage in her life.

Many worthwhile texts give guidance for working with our dreams and for establishing group formats. One example is *Where People Fly and Rivers Run Uphill* by Jeremy Taylor.[6] Those who wish to pay attention to dreams as a tool for releasing barriers to growth can discover encouragement and clarity hidden in these nighttime scenarios.

Scripture

We call it the "Living Word of God," but we often treat the Bible as if it were dead, rigid, and locked in a culture with strange customs and detached language. Bible teacher Hazelyn McComas, a highly respected presenter at the Academy for Spiritual Formation, views Scripture as a place where we encounter the Living God. She regards the stories as attempts to express the inexpressible through metaphor, hyperbole, and imagination. Approached with heartfelt openness, these ancient messages can speak directly to our point of need, *exposing the barriers and lifting them to awareness.* This exercise is an example:

1. Relax your body. Sit in a comfortable chair, taking several deep breaths, breathing in *calm* and breathing out *anxiety.* Continue sitting in silence for a few moments.

2. Read the Exodus story, the dramatic parting of the Red Sea found in Exod 14. The children of Israel have been slaves to the Egyptians, living in bondage for many generations. They are yearning for the Promised Land. But the Red Sea forms a barrier that seems impenetrable. Miraculously, the seas part, and Moses leads them to freedom.

3. Reflect on what God may be saying to you as you read the passage and ask yourself: What holds me in bondage? What is my barrier to freedom—my Red Sea? From what do I need deliverance? What is the freedom to which God may be inviting me?

4. Respond by offering your reflection to God in prayer. You may wish to journal your insights.

5. Rest in God's presence, being open to God's word for you.

I must admit that I've always had an ambivalent relationship with the Psalms, on the one hand revering them as the prayer book of Jesus himself, and on the other hand appalled at their vindictive passages. My responses were imbedded in memories of countless Sunday mornings, as an impressionable young girl reading words from the Psalms, often as responsive liturgical readings, such as "I have nothing but hatred for them; I count them my enemies" (Ps 139:22), or "you will dash them to pieces like pottery" (Ps 2:9b). These texts were read with no context and no explanation, with the inference that they were the "words of God." As a result, my theology was deformed by a misunderstanding of the Psalter.

Again, Hazelyn McComas was God's instrument of change for me. She presented the psalm prayers as honest, often raw, communication with God from the depths of human experience. The writers laugh, cry, praise, lament, complain, demand—just like we do. The psalmists write from two assumptions, says McComas: first, that God *is,* and second, that God is *with us.* Through praying the Psalms, we can release our deepest feelings in uncensored relationship with God, who knows our hearts anyway.

The tradition of the psalmists can also lead us to write our own prayers, not only of praise and adoration, but also of protest and lament. My friend, Carol, an only child who had been struggling with the care of her mother in the maze of Alzeimer's, wrote the following lament:

Lament for Ruby

O God, where can you be?

My life continues in misery, my speech reduced to stammers, my former joys and wisdom reduced to faint glimpses of what I used to be.

Where do you abide, O God, while I shrink and fade, my voice of praise now only unintelligible murmurs, my strong legs in a lifetime of working now unsteady, shuffling lumps that impede my every movement, my still bright smile accompanied by empty eyes searching for help?

O God, oh holy creator of all my joys, my lifetime of mountains to climb and hillsides to joyously slide down, maker of my precious loved ones who also guide and travel with me, designer of my laughter and great energies to work among the nations, teacher of steadfast hope in all my losses, my sustainer in the wars with my enemies—where are you now?

O God, whisperer of hope within,

Why do you ignore me? Why do you look past my suffering? Why do you prolong my living? Am I not worthy of the prize of death?

Hear me, O God. Allow the messenger of death to bring release from the wicked captivity that I may again be whole in my life with you.

Carol described the overwhelming sense of peace that engulfed her after she poured out her frustration on paper—the feeling of a heavy burden released. The laments of the psalmist connected her to her own deep lament and became for her a precious tool of letting go.

For Reflection

1. Honestly examine your prayer life. Is it mostly asking for things? What might you do to develop your skills in listening to God?

2. Meditate on the Scripture, "Be still and know that I am God" (Ps 46:10). Take five minutes for each of the following:

   - Be still and know that I am God.

   - Be still and know that I am

   - Be still and know that I

   - Be still and know

● Be still

● Be . . .

Journal about your insights to each phrase as you listen to God.

3. Do you recall your dreams? Are there recurrent themes? If you wish to pursue dreamwork as a spiritual tool, try keeping a pen and paper next to your bed so that you can record your dreams when you first wake up.

11

Availability

Ask, and it shall be given to you; seek, and you shall find; knock, and it shall be opened to you. (Matt 7:7)

Those who wait for the Lord shall renew their strength, they shall mount up with wings like eagles, they shall run and not be weary, they shall walk and not faint. (Isa 40:31)

As we took our companionable walk around the neighborhood, I stole a glance at Nancy's tight-lipped profile. Eyes ahead, jaw clenched in consternation. I could tell that she was chewing on a thought, that something was dogging her. A devout woman of intellect and integrity, she obviously had a bee in her bonnet that wouldn't stop buzzing. Something was out of sync, churning inside. She knew that her emotions were out of kilter, fueled by exasperation at her ex-husband. The *awareness* was there, but she couldn't budge any further.

As a counselor herself, Nancy knew the importance of letting go. She knew she needed to get rid of her anger, but—try as she might—her rage refused to respond to her well-intentioned commands. Knowing what to do and doing it were two different things. One part of her told the anger to go away; the other part held on stubbornly, wanting to experience her righteous indignation just a little longer. After all, she had clearly been wronged and didn't want to release her sense of victimization. Yet, the burden of it was weighing her down.

Finally, she sighed and shook her head in frustration, "I can't do this forgiveness thing by myself. My feelings are too bruised, too tender. I know I need divine power to assist me, but my prayers for help are not really sincere. I'm not sure I'm honestly ready to let it go. The best I can say right now is that I'm willing to be willing."

That courageously honest admission kept her in the game. She was making herself *available* for the next healing step—even if it was a baby step.

Sometimes a tiny opening in the heart is all you can manage, so it makes sense to begin where you are, how you are. Don't wait until you feel like it; don't wait until you have it all figured out; don't wait until you're good enough.

Scripture tells us to "knock and it shall be opened." Making ourselves *available* is the rapping of our knuckles on the door. Author Wayne Dyer said it beautifully in *The Power of Intention*: "The assistance you need will be provided by the universe as you convert your readiness to willingness."[1]

Wise teacher Flora Wuellner, in *Forgiveness, the Passionate Journey*, images the process not as one we produce, but rather an existing force that we enter: "Ultimately, forgiveness is not our power at all but God's power flowing toward us, in us, through us, like a mighty river."[2]

If you can't jump into that flowing force now, perhaps you're ready to stick a toe in. Here are some practices that can make you available to the cleansing current that can wash away resistance.

Support

Nancy said with clarity, "The only way I can go on is to see someone else who has gone on." It's hard to overstate the power of a supportive network of those who have been there. Admitting that we need to release something—whether it's a habit, a hang-up, or a human being—invites us to take a step toward vulnerability. That vulnerability makes us *available*. Without it, we can continue in our rigidity, professing that we don't have a problem.

Years ago, Alcoholics Anonymous pioneered the concept of group encouragement and accountability and has been an agent of change in the lives of millions. It has become the prototype for dozens of support groups that offer advice and a comforting sense of solidarity with others in the same boat. Recovery groups of all kinds abound in churches, community centers, and hospital settings. They serve to facilitate one's availability to the experienced reflection of others. Plus, it eases the feeling of loneliness and futility that can be paralyzing to growth.

In some instances, there is no substitute for individual counseling or personal therapy. Thankfully, the stigma that society has long attached to the need for psychological help is dissipating. In my growing-up years, counseling was usually seen as a sign of weakness—or worse still, a lack of faith. There was an unspoken assumption that "real Christians" should rely on God, not psychology. Unfortunately, that prevented many from getting the professional help that could have made a difference. Surely caring professionals could embody God's gifts of healing.

As a friend told me off-handedly, "The way I see it, if the washing machine is broken, I call an experienced repairman. So, if my emotional system seems out of whack, doesn't it make sense to talk to someone who is trained in those matters?" Sounds reasonable to me. It's another way of making ourselves *available* to wise input.

Support comes in many packages, sometimes in unlikely ones. Sensitive friends often intuit what we need to aid our healing even when we are unable to ask. They love us enough to put themselves in our shoes long enough to ask the question, "What would really help?" When possible, we need to surround ourselves with friends who build us up, not drag us down.

Sometimes just the fact that friends *show up* speaks volumes to our vulnerable spirits. In *Let Your Life Speak*, Parker Palmer speaks candidly of his experience of deep depression. He relates this visit from a friend: "Blessedly, there were several people who had the courage to stand with me in a simple and healing way. One of them was a friend named Bill who, having asked my permission to do so, stopped by my home every afternoon, sat me down in a chair, knelt in front of me, removed my shoes and socks, and for half an hour simply massaged my feet."[3]

I recall a similar incident many years ago. Two friends came to my aid when I was too confused and disturbed to articulate my needs. It was the day my divorce was finalized. My sons were with their grandmother, and I had been away all day working in another city. Weary with fatigue, I came home to my big *empty* two-story house in unspeakable despair. On my kitchen table was a note written on the back of a torn brown grocery sack.

1. On the top shelf of the refrigerator is a turkey sandwich. Eat it.

2. On the second shelf is a glass of wine. Drink it.

3. Go upstairs.

I recognized the handwriting as that of a dear friend. She and another friend had found the key that I kept hidden under a flowerpot and let themselves into my house, which smelled of furniture polish and pine-scented cleanser and was sparkling clean—a far cry from the mess I had left that morning.

When I climbed the stairs, I saw the fresh linens on my bed, neatly turned back, hotel-style, with a chocolate on the pillow and a silky nightgown laid out carefully on top of the covers. A rose bloomed in a vase on the bedside table. Inside the bathroom were more pampering pleasures. Scented bath oil, a lavender candle—even matches—sat on the rim of the tub. Another note instructed, "Run a tub full of water, pour in oil, get in it. Then put on the nightgown and get in bed. We love you." I followed their directions like a robot, feeling their loving support enfolding me like a warm, cuddly blanket. The tender thoughtfulness of their actions still brings tears to my eyes twenty-five years later, and the memory continues to sustain me. You can be sure that the note, scribbled hurriedly on a scrap of brown paper, is in my treasure box—honored like the priceless heirloom that it is.

All too often, loving friends yearn to support and help us, but we persist in claiming (falsely), "I'm just fine. I don't need anything," wearing our faltering independence like a badge of honor. Actually, it's a mark of maturity to be able to ask for what we need and receive *graciously*. In other words, we give others the gift of being able to embody their concern and support. Such actions on our part don't make us *weak*, they make us *real*.

Study

I once heard someone refer to books as "portable pastors"—a vehicle of ministry that travels where human beings may not be welcome. Most of us have experienced the life-giving resonance when we read the right word at the right time—a healing balm that makes us *available* to fresh insights.

The bookstores overflow with materials that can facilitate our freedom— titles too numerous to list. One text that propels many Christians along the path of release is *Praying Our Goodbyes* by Joyce Rupp.[4]

She chronicles many experiences of leaving behind and moving ahead, then ends the book with no less than twenty-four prayers, designed for specific circumstances: "Prayer for a Lonely Day," "Prayer of One Who Feels Broken Apart," "Prayer to Regain One's Inner Strength," "Prayer of One Who Is Moving On," "Prayer of One Terminating a Relationship," "Prayer For Trust When Experiencing a Loss" and others. The prayers are accompanied by useful images, scriptural references, and precise suggestions. It's a useful handbook of letting-go exercises.

The Artist's Way by Julia Cameron speaks in a somewhat different language, geared to the release of blocks to creativity. A book to be done rather than read, it offers particular tasks and tools for accessing the creative child that exists in every one of us. By uncovering the harmful messages of the past and the negative influences of the present, the reader can not only unlock buried talents such as painting and writing, but also can begin to approach *life* as a creative enterprise—lived in tandem with God's creative power. Besides being able to excavate the sources of blocked artistry, the book is just plain fun. I've been involved in studies of *The Artist's Way* both as a facilitator and as a student, and I have been amazed at its power to get people unstuck in a playful, step-by-step manner—a remarkably transformative text.

Many women in search of authenticity have benefited from the study of Sue Monk Kidd's *When the Heart Waits*. As she candidly catalogs her own journey to wholeness, readers are invited to put their lives under a spiritual microscope, examining crippling thought forms and ways of being that need to be discarded or transformed. Because of its sound psychological and spiritual base, it is a powerful wake-up call to those seeking to live life honestly. When I read it for the first time, I felt as if someone were looking over my shoulder and into my secret thoughts. Kidd has a gift for articulating the inner life of women that opens our eyes, making us available for change.

In *The Heart of Christianity*,[5] Marcus Borg re-visits Christian thought and doctrine in ways that can help us thoughtfully explore what we believe. Many of us are reluctant to face the fragile foundation of some religious dogma without an experienced guide, and this book provides a way to enter that territory.

Borg's clear, accessible style and winsome way of sharing his own doubts conveys a sense of safety that, frankly, made me willing to risk bringing some of my buried questions to the light of serious scrutiny. In a church group study setting, it is a potent tool for discussion and community-building, whether one agrees with every single word of it or not. It at least gets the issues on the table.

Subscribe to several church newsletters to check out the educational opportunities they offer. Pay attention to community offerings, library events, public lectures. Wisdom and light can come flooding in when one has the courage to fearlessly open the window of the heart.

Story

A wise-looking elderly woman approached me as the seminar ended. The three-day lecture series had ended on a positive note, and I hoped that my presentations had been well organized and well received. However, this woman definitely had something on her mind—she was someone on a mission with a message.

"Pardon me, young woman," she began (she was about eighty and I was somewhere in my fifties). "I feel there is something I ought to tell you."

I braced myself.

"Your talks were fine—nothing wrong with them," she said almost apologetically. Then she added, "But you need to tell more stories. Now those two things that happened with your kids—we *got* it when you told what you experienced. We'll remember that; but frankly, we may forget the rest of it."

Smiling, I thanked her and realized I had just been given an important lesson in human nature, not to mention public speaking. I had been schooled in the notion that to talk about oneself, to relate one's own experiences, was inappropriate and self-serving. So I'd always been careful to keep personal references to a minimum. This woman's astute and honest remarks gave me a different perspective, and I gained a deep respect for the power of story.

Part of making ourselves *available* to change involves connecting to the portions of other people's experiences that contain a golden nugget for us. We are alerted to those things by the feeling of deep inner resonance that usually occurs in the body without our controlling or directing it. What moved us to tears? What made our ears perk up? When did we find ourselves leaning forward in our seat? What gave us the thought, "She must have read my mind?" What gave us that overwhelming sense of "Me, too!" Those kinds of reactions should startle us into deeper investigation—because there's a message in there for us. It can lead us to deeper questions, such as, "What tender wound did the story touch? What is unhealed in me? What pushed my buttons? Why?"

In addition to the countless contemporary tales of loss, Bible stories have a unique power to connect us with the next step, giving us the nudge we need. However, to engage Scripture for *trans*formation, rather than simply *in*formation, we must enter the story in an imaginative way. Read it as if for the first time, picturing yourself as one of the characters. Allow the story to become your own as you superimpose it on your life situation and let it speak to you. Holy Scripture offers an array of timeless truths bound up in parables and human sagas.

Growing up in the forties and fifties meant hearing Bible stories weekly, usually illustrated with colorful flannel-board figures. I learned the narratives, but my connection was as an observer, learning about long-ago events in a culture that seemed eons away from my own experience. Though I became very familiar with all the action, it was about someone else, not me.

That changed surprisingly when I encountered a different form of biblical study as an adult. As a young mother of two sons—a kindergartner and a fourth-grader—I felt my brain turning to jelly, so I decided to go to school, too. Since Lambuth College, a small United Methodist college in Jackson, Tennessee, was just a few blocks away, I indulged my religious curiosity by enrolling in a Bible survey course taught by Dr. Paul Blankenship. It lit my fire in a way I could not have predicted. I couldn't wait from one class to the next. I was riveted to the lectures, in which the Bible was approached with intellectual rigor as well as reverence—a combination I had yearned for. Later biblical studies, taught by Dr. Gene Davenport, continued to infuse the Scriptures with vitality, significance, and a lively heartbeat.

But it was the story of Job that introduced me to the *living Word*, rather than an interesting, ancient document. Our final semester assignment was to write an essay on the meaning of the Job story. We were urged to move into the text, and I plunged headlong into the action-packed narrative. I read Archibald MacLeish's play, *J. B.*[6] I combed the commentaries. I studied the details of Job's plight as he was stripped of everything he had—possessions, beliefs, family, friends, health. The question, "Why?" leapt off the pages in verse after verse, tragedy after tragedy. His story was the epitome of the struggle to know, the determination to be right, the search for the answer.

Mysteriously, somewhere along the way, his story became my own. I exhausted every cognitive argument I could muster until finally—along with Job—I had to admit that "the answer is that there is no answer." It was probably the first time I had even begun to comprehend the Mystery of God in a visceral way. When everything had been taken from Job, all he had left was *God*. Though God didn't resolve his need to know, Job ultimately became content just to be in the divine relationship. It was enough for Job, and I found that it was enough for me, too.

A clever friend told me once that Bible stories aren't meant to be third-class mail marked "Occupant," but rather first-class mail marked "Personal." Through Bible studies that strive for transformation rather than information, we can escape the rigid systems of study that keep us in a box. This tends to expand us into growth rather than constrict us into stagnation. It seems to me that most studies approach the Bible like a multiple-choice test, determined to discern the "right" interpretation—a, b, c, or d. The Bible as the living, breathing, dynamic Word of God contains layers of meaning. It can mean "all of the above." It can become for us a place where we are made *available* to the Mystery of God.

For example, let's take a look at the familiar verse from the Lord's Prayer, found in Matt 6:11: "Give us this day, our daily bread."

- If I am a struggling victim in a refugee camp, that prayer could be for literal bread.

- If I am celebrating the Eucharist, it can represent the bread of the Lord's Supper.

- If I am reading the Scriptures, it can refer to the spiritual food that feeds the soul—the Word of God.

- If I am seeking closer communion with Jesus, this bread can also refer to Jesus as "the bread of life" in John 6:33–35.

- If I am steeped in Jewish tradition, the mention of daily bread might honor a belief in the Messianic Banquet, a time when God would call the people to a feast in the Kingdom of God.

The point is not which interpretation is right, but whether, as a living Word, the Bible can speak to our individual needs and situations. I would like to believe that this sacred text is bigger and broader and richer than our limited ability to comprehend or categorize it.

In that context, we can make ourselves *available* to the timeless truths of Bible stories. There's the story of Mary, the mother of Jesus, and her supreme abandonment of self. There's Paul, whose letters are filled with his battles to let go of legalism in the service of the law of love. There's Jonah, whose stubbornness led him to the belly of the whale, where he at last discarded his narrow agenda. And there are lots more where those came from.

Sacred texts, fairy tales, anecdotes—as well as our neighbor's tale of woe—offer us rich reservoirs of truth to be tapped. We are created with a capacity to be touched and taught through the sharing of experiences. No wonder my grandchild's first sentence to me was "Lindy, tell me a story . . ."

Sorrow

Sometimes tragedy and sorrow literally propel us into *availability* with a force unlike anything else. Events can broadside us with such devastating power that there is no way to return to life as it was. We're required to rearrange all the shattered fragments that once looked like a normal existence.

The unspeakable happened to my friend Ellen. She found her precious seven-year old Rebecca dead in a small amount of bathwater on a run-of-the-mill family evening. Weeks later, they discovered that Rebecca had been the victim of a rare condition called Cornelia de Lange, but no matter the cause, she was gone. The sudden loss of this vibrant, happy presence left a gaping hole of profound sorrow in the life of Rebecca's family, as well as in the relational orbit of each individual member.

Ellen was willing to share some of her insights, gleaned during deliberate periods of reflection in the months following Rebecca's death. After the flurry of those first weeks, she committed to carving out a sacred space for specific grief work—at least one full "grief day" a month, spent at a retreat center or other quiet space. During this day, she remembered Rebecca, honored her life, wrote in her journal, cried, laughed, entered the grief as completely as she could. However, she found that even with persistent effort, there was a stubborn thread of resistance to letting Rebecca go. Part of her didn't really want to let go.

"If I let go," she explained, "I won't have her in my life anymore, and I want to keep her!" As time went by, she realized that it was more a matter of reincorporating her relationship with Rebecca than releasing it. Ellen had let go of carpool, doctor's appointments, and school events, but she was understandably clinging fiercely to her daughter. She concluded, "I began to see that even though Rebecca no longer needed a mother, I still needed a daughter. I had to find a way to let go in a different way—to let go of the relationship *as I had originally defined it* and find a meaningful way of continuing to be her mother."

She discovered that the deep grief work was not to be found in cognitive understanding, but in being *available* to fresh insights. She was fed by the time-honored rituals of Judaism and found their prescriptive rites of mourning behavior to be not only nourishing, but also deeply grounding. She read a number of inspiring books, but she singled out *Finding Hope When a Child Dies* as the most helpful.[7]

Ellen searched for specific ways to expand her mothering role. In addition to deepening her relationships with her two older children, she found that she could make a difference in the lives of other young girls. She preferred to perform anonymous acts of charity, which placed no burden of thanks on the recipient, but served her own need to nurture. Even the periodic donation of blood seemed enormously healing. She gave herself permission to be childlike and outrageously playful—just as Rebecca had been. She availed herself of any number of tools for integrating her grief—music, personal ritual, dreams—accepting all of them as gifts for her healing process.

Over a period of months, a beautiful transition took place. Grief became her friend, rather than her taskmaster. She entered what she called "a chain of sisters," women who had also lost a child and were giving meaning to their sorrow by befriending one another. Part of the healing, she discovered, was embracing the opportunity to "adopt" another woman and continue the chain of caring ministry, being vulnerable to the pain and suffering of another.

Ellen had become *aware* of her need to let go through the natural God-given process of grief. In prayer and reflection, she became *available* to new wisdom. Then she embodied those insights by taking *action*.

For Reflection

1. Choose a Bible story that intrigues or inspires you. Read it slowly twice, seeing yourself as one of the characters. Spend some quiet time in meditation, making yourself available to the personal wisdom it may hold for you.

2. Is there a situation in your past where circumstances made you available to the wisdom you needed?

3. What is one activity or situation you might choose that would facilitate your ability to access the information or inspiration you need?

Action

Therefore, since we are surrounded by so great a cloud of witnesses, let us also lay aside every weight and the sin that clings so closely, and let us run with perseverance the race that is set before us. (Heb 12:1)

Imagine that you're standing at the edge of a deep, dark forest. You want desperately to reach the other side to freedom, but you don't know exactly how to navigate it. It looks daunting, scary, perhaps even impossible, but you're committed to the journey. And all you have in your jeans pocket is a tiny flashlight.

Then imagine a Voice giving you encouragement and instructions:

- Take out your flashlight and shine it on the path before you.

- Step into that small circle of light that you can see.

- Shine the flashlight forward again.

- If you stumble and fall, simply smile and breathe a forgiving "oops!"

    (No guilt and remorse allowed; it's a waste of time.)

- Dust yourself off and get back on the path.

- Repeat process again, and again, and again.

- You will reach the other side, one point of light at a time.

In other words, *act* on the light you have now. It doesn't have to be the final word, the clearest word, or the most profound word. You don't have to wait until the situation improves or until you feel like it. The road to release doesn't have to be laid out on a meticulous map. In fact, knowledge of the path is no substitute for placing one foot in front of the other. You simply proceed with the light you have been given through your *awareness and availability*. Take a risk and *act*.

Oddly enough, people usually think that taking action involves directly fixing a problem, finding a solution. However, in the process of letting go, that is often counterproductive. The procedure seems to be best served by registering the intention of letting go, then somehow aligning oneself with positive, life-giving energy and *acting* in cooperation with God's healing power to make us whole. God is always inviting us to step beyond where we are. It's a bit like putting your canoe into a swift river and going with the current. You still have to paddle, but you're being supported by a force much greater than you and your little boat.

C. S. Lewis wrote in *The Problem of Pain* that "the doors of hell are locked from the inside."[1] While it is true that we acknowledge our dependence on a power outside ourselves to light our path, or float our boat, we must be willing to do our part. God will not arbitrarily force us to relinquish that which we refuse to release.

Here are a few suggestions to help you get into the flow of that healing current.

Creativity

It's no surprise that, as children of a Creator God, we seem to be hardwired for creativity. We participate in our own transformation every time we respond to that creative urge placed within each one of us. "But, I'm not creative!" we protest, always pointing to the painters, sculptors, musicians, and writers as the "talented" ones. But we can't let ourselves off the hook that easily. Just because the creative child within us is ignored and neglected doesn't mean that child doesn't exist! Life offers us a limitless number of choices to honor that basic instinct to shape, to sing, to generate. As Auntie Mame so cleverly put it in a memorable scene from the famous musical comedy, "Life is a banquet, and most poor [souls] are starving to death!"[2]

Obviously, this instinctive need to create is a part of how God made us. Whether we're rearranging furniture, playing a game of "Pretend" with the children, shaping a business plan, or filling a canvas with paint, we're exercising a life-giving part of ourselves. In some mysterious way, this creative energy has the capacity to heal and transform us in every area of our lives, and that includes the process of letting go.

Gardening
No wonder the parables of Jesus abound with earthy images of fields and flowers, planting and plowing—nature's silent reminders of letting go. My neighbor Henry loves to putter in the garden and finds countless metaphors when he needs to let go of something. . . .

- Henry can till the soil of his soul through meditative prayer, readying it for new growth.

- He can pull up the weeds of resistance as they appear.

- He can carefully plant seeds of hope and transformation.

- He can regularly rake away old hurts and habits.

- He can water and nurture the sprouts of newness.

- He can celebrate the emergence of new fruits and flowers.

Most of all, Henry can sit quietly on a bench in his garden, trusting that a greater power is working unseen through rain and sunshine as well as beneath the soil. He knows he can't make those plants flourish under his own limited power, but must trust a hidden energy outside himself whose very nature is Creation.

Cooking

Madeline cooks her way to creativity. As she chops and dices, stirs and slices, she sorts out the elements of her life as well as the Brunswick stew. She prays for a harmonious blend, seeing what ingredients will contribute to the whole and what will make it distasteful. What flavor needs to be more spicy? More colorful? Less dominating? What needs to be eliminated from the mixture? Every whiff of the new creation carries an appreciation for the work in progress—on the stove and in her soul.

Weaving

My sister Anita, an accomplished weaver, uses her craft to remind her of the "weaving together of mind, body, and spirit into the tapestry of life." Weavers can't always be sure of the outcome as they interlace yarns and threads together. As the colors interact with one another, their combined characteristics change the hues and emerge as a creative surprise. At some point, she tells me, good weavers let go of their original concept to some degree and allow the threads to weave their own magic. What a meaningful metaphor for releasing our plans and agendas.

Hands-on creative pursuits seem to enter a kind of mysterious realm in which the body moves us toward wholeness, even when the mind and spirit may be lagging behind. The activity itself urges us forward, inviting the soul to unfold in ways that are hard to describe. However, as I see evidence of it— again and again—in the lives of those around me, I am eager to affirm its "magic" even if I don't completely understand it.

Knitting

> For it was you who formed my inward parts; you knit me together in my mother's womb. (Ps 139:13)

Knitting has been credited with turning out beautiful souls as well as sweaters. It's slow, it's process-oriented, it's meditative. Each stitch can be a symbol for letting go. In the thoughtful book, *Zen and the Art of Knitting*,[3] author Bernadette Murphy identifies a number of metaphorical uses for the craft, including letting go of perfectionism. Through knitting, she explains, she is learning to embrace the spirituality of imperfection. Sometimes one must accept the irregularity of a stitch gone awry and allow it to be part of the whole.

On other occasions, knitting can represent the need to let go of the chaos of life (scattered and separate yarns) and bring order and design to it. The pattern can represent the emerging pattern of a more integrated life, a reminder of the web of existence, the interconnectedness of all things.

Author and knitter Susan Jorgensen makes this observation in the beautiful book, *Knitting Into the Mystery*: "Something more is at work in the shawls that we knit, something more than knit three, purl three. The totality of the shawl is more than the sum of the knitter, the wearer, and the yarn, and is something that we can't possess. Mystery invites us simply to attend to it, to relish in it, to savor the flow and feel of yarn over fingers, of shawl over shoulders."[4]

So grab a ball of yarn and take *action*.

Pottery

Ancient scriptural texts appreciate the richness of pottery as a representation of spiritual transformation. Isaiah 64:8 images God as the one who forms us: "... we are the clay; you are our potter; we are all the work of your hand." In Jer 18:4, we are reminded that God can take an imperfect vessel and mold it anew: "The vessel he was making of clay was spoiled in the potter's hand, and he reworked it into another vessel, as seemed good to him." Scores of potters today find this tactile art form a symbol of co-creating with God, of seeing something useful and beautiful emerge from a formless lump of muddiness.

Episcopal preacher and writer John Claypool wrote about the divine molding process in *Mending the Heart*.[5] He spoke of it as "a process of patient trial and error" in which "God is more interested in the future than the past, more concerned about what we can still become than what we used to be ... God is not a perfectionist, but a merciful nurturer." God is a potter we can trust with the molding of our souls.

While it seems that the events in our lives shape us, it is actually the spirit in which we experience those events that molds us most deeply. As Rev. Steve Garnas-Holmes explained in one of his newsletters, "We cannot always choose what we experience, but we can choose how we experience it."[6] We can let go of our own frantic attempts to shape ourselves and trust the divine Potter's hands of love and gentleness, trust and respect, hope and delight.

Perhaps "throwing a pot" can remind us of that.

Decorating and Renovation

Polly embraced the renovation of her new home as a metaphor for the renovation of her life. Feeling herself overwhelmed by the chaotic, unending tasks involved in such an undertaking, she made the decision to use the situation as a vehicle for spiritual growth, rather than succumbing to incessant complaining. She discarded the things she no longer needed, letting them go freely. She examined her long-held inhibitions about what colors one "ought" to use and let her imagination and intuition guide her. The landscaping brought her deeply in touch with the inspirations of nature. Through liturgies of house blessings, she asked God to bless each new space with love and kindness. In other words, she approached the repainting and rebuilding in a soulful manner, acting to not only redecorate her house, but also her life. She entered the sacred rhythm of loss and gain.

Music
I can hardly find words to convey the magic of music in shaping the soul. We need to be intentional about *acting* to surround ourselves with its healing balm. Performers and listeners alike seem to participate in the awesome transformative power, whether as creator or receiver. And by some strange miracle, it helps us let go.

A few years ago at a church conference in Dallas, I witnessed one of those miracles. The occasion was a stimulating theological think-tank event where the best and the brightest were discussing the fine points of theology in a rarified academic atmosphere. I was a silent observer, trying my best to keep up with the intellectual debate and having a tough time of it. My brow was furrowed all week long. However, even though it pushed me to the brink of brainpower, it challenged me in a way that I found absolutely delicious. It was the theological equivalent of eating a box of Godiva chocolates.

I slid into the pew at the closing worship service with my mind saturated and my spirit enlivened. Given the kind of week it had been (how many angels can dance on the head of a pin?), I was expecting a little Handel and Bach with a formal liturgy—strictly high-church. The special music was being provided by an African-American contralto with an outstanding local reputation, and I was hoping she would sing something familiar from *The Messiah*. After the intellectual workout of the previous days, I felt my over-taxed brain couldn't absorb a musical challenge on top of everything else.

To everyone's surprise, the musical offering took an unexpected turn. The musician sat at the piano, accompanying herself, and hit one simple chord of introduction. Then her magnificent voice filled the room, "Jesus *loves* me, this I know, for the Bible tells me so. . . ." Then with a change of keys and tempo, she began again, "Jesus *loves* me, this I know. . . ." Then yet another rhythm and range, "Jesus loves *me*, this I know. . . ." And finally, "Jesus loves me, *this I know.*"

You could have heard a pin drop in that sanctuary filled with PhD's and professors, many searching for a hankie in the pocket of their three-piece suits. It was as if all the theological posturing had been let go in the face of the loving power that united all of us. After the dogma had been debated and the ink had dried on all the presentation papers, a simple children's chorus reminded us that "the greatest of these is love."

Music is vital to spiritual health and has transformative powers that can bring grace and simplicity to our complex lives. It touches something higher in us and becomes the agent of a special kind of divine therapy. Writer Karen Armstrong describes the power of music to ease transitions and open the soul: "[I was] almost shocked by the beauty of the slow movement of Beethoven's Emperor Concerto. While I listened, I felt my spirit knitting together. Things began to make sense."[7]

Author Cynthia Bourgeault conveys a similar sentiment in *The Wisdom Way of Knowing*. She speaks of becoming "a string in the concert of God's joy. I am 'sounded through' by the music, and in that sounding, in harmonic resonance with all the other instruments, is revealed both my irreplaceable uniqueness and my inescapable belonging."[8]

Art

When I consider examples of the alchemy of art, I always think first of writer Henri Nouwen's life-changing encounter with Rembrandt's famous painting, *The Return of the Prodigal Son*.[9] In fact, the experience was so powerful for Nouwen that he wrote an entire book about its impact on his life. He was able to let go of years of addiction to the opinions of others and release his control over his own spiritual journey, inspired by the sight of the prodigal in the arms of the loving Father. As he identified also with the elder brother in the parable, he was moved to face and release his own feelings of rivalry and competition.

I know how he feels. My favorite painting is by artist Lendon Noe of Jackson, Tennessee. It hangs in a prominent spot in my home and urges me toward authenticity every time I look at it. I bought it in the midst of a painful transition and it grabbed me in my gut like no other painting ever has. It is a contemporary rendering of a faceless woman, seated cross-legged and straining upward, reaching for something beyond herself, yet within herself. At least that was what I saw when I first spied it in the window of a gallery. Owning it is like having a sacred icon in the house.

That triggers the memory of an incident that first taught me about the power of art to move the human spirit. It happened more than thirty years ago on a whirlwind tour of Italy where our group of thirty-somethings were on an inexpensive college alumni tour. We were travel-weary and thoroughly saturated with the richness of Italian art (and food) as we trudged off the bus in Florence to tour yet another art museum. Of all the travelers, Gayle was probably the most composed—the epitome of control. Though she was fun-loving, she wasn't given to emotional outbursts of any kind. In fact, I don't think I had ever seen her "lose it." But as we stood in a circle around Michelangelo's massive sculpture of David, I saw her slowly and silently sink to the cold marble floor on her knees and begin to sob.

It was a gift—a gift of artistic power that was unexpected, undeserved, and involuntary. As I observed her that day, her reliable composure reduced to rubble, I knew I was in the presence of a sacred moment. In some mysterious way, art and music have the capacity to touch our hearts in hidden places where words can't reach us.

So, take up creative pursuits. Attend a concert. Spend quality time at a museum. Those might not seem like obvious tools for letting go, but they are. As we become *aware* of our need to let go and see to become *available* to new wisdom, we must *act* to place ourselves in contact with these creative sources of the sacred.

Transforming Thought

> . . . . whatever is true, whatever is honorable, whatever is just, whatever is pure, whatever is pleasing, whatever is commendable, if there is any excellence and if there is anything worthy of praise, think about these things. (Phil 4:8)

You are what you think. I used to snub my nose at such a simplistic saying, dismissing it as new-age jargon. After all, doesn't the universe hurl comets at us? Doesn't life dole out pain and pleasure at random? Aren't most life events beyond our control? Obviously, I don't hold the answers to cosmic dilemmas, but I'm willing to admit that I've changed my mind about *changing my mind*. I'm beginning to agree with speaker and author Wayne Dyer, who remarked on public television, "When you change the way you look at things, the things you look at change."[10]

Years of observing my own life and the lives of others (plus metaphysics and perennial wisdom) have led me to believe that what we focus on gets bigger. In many ways, belief creates our reality from the inside out, not from the outside in. Phrases such as "change your thinking; change your life" may be sweeping generalizations, it's true, but they contain fundamental truths that we ignore at our peril.

So what does this have to do with letting go? Everything. It means that *the most significant action we can take is an internal one.* If there is something I want to release, something that I do not want mirrored in my life, I must find a way not to dwell on it. (As previously stated, this step comes after the feelings have been felt and acknowledged adequately.) If I perpetuate, attract, and manifest that which I think about, then it behooves me to become attentive to the workings of my own mind.

Does this mean that I will ignore problems and predicaments or pretend that evil doesn't exist? No. I can acknowledge the presence of evil, of despair, of heartache, but I can choose not to live there permanently. Simplistic? Maybe. Effective? You bet. My worry and desperation can't do one single thing to solve hardships on a personal or a global level; in fact, my malaise may instead hinder me from effective efforts of compassion. The fretting space inside us can be replaced with something infinitely healthier.

Even our prayers can reflect an intentionally positive mindset, one that shows more compassion and less self-judgment. For example, our petition,

"Dear Lord, please abolish and control my terrible temper," can be restated as "Help me to be the loving person that reflects your Spirit of love and compassion." This reframes and redirects the negative energy. It's always an inside job.

The Greek word *metanoia* appears frequently throughout the Bible and is commonly translated *repentance* or *change of mind*, implying some sort of alteration of thought that leads to salvation or wholeness. This kind of transformative mind change is an indication of God's saving grace.

But we must cooperate with this divine intention. God will not haul us kicking and screaming into the kingdom nor bring us to wholeness against our will. What, then, is our part of the bargain? Once again, awareness is the beginning point, but it needs decisive action. What thoughts dominate our minds? What reactions drive us unconsciously?

It's necessary to get very, very specific. Our tendency is to speak in broad intentions, such as "I've got to do better—I'm supposed be more optimistic." This broad-brush, judgmental approach is a bit like telling a child, "You *be good*, do you hear?!" rather than "Tommy, let's talk about what happens when you hit your sister."

So what would such action look like? It begins with paying attention to your thoughts, not in an accusatory way as if you're primed to do battle with them, but in a gentle, watchful manner, paying close attention to the seeds that are unconsciously planted. Learn to recognize the negative lens when you begin to don that familiar pair of gray glasses. For instance, let's suppose you're part of a group discussion when your mind grabs center stage: "Why are we doing this? Why did he say that stupid thing? She sure did look at me strangely—I wonder what's wrong with her? This room is too hot anyway. That was a dumb remark I made. I'll bet everyone thinks I'm an idiot." And the automatic evaluating and judgment take off like a runaway train, bound for frustration, ill temper, grumpiness, anger, even depression.

Your task is to train yourself, one thought at a time, to spot the process and stop it. "Aha, there it is again. . . . the negative lens," you might say to yourself. When you discover the negativity, rather than a self-deprecating "Oh, no, I've done it again—when will I learn?" let your internal dialog stem from a surge of gratitude—gratitude for the awareness that led you to specific information, to *action*. Don't get into a debate with yourself about the goodness and badness of your thoughts. Simply acknowledge them, take a deep breath, and have compassion for the part of yourself that is reactive and fearful. Spotting a negative thought can be a bit like waving at an old friend, but one you don't want to take to the movies anymore!

Your mind isn't in control of you; you are in control of your mind. You can expect your mind to prattle on and on—that's what minds are prone to do. Rather than engaging in a war with your own thoughts, accept the chatter instead of criticizing it. When a negative thought arises say, "I hear you, but I'm moving on; you're no longer in charge of me." In that way, you aren't denying its presence, neither are you giving your power over to the dark thought. You can never be free while constantly rehearsing a failing future. Acknowledge the thought, let it go, and move beyond it. Calm the mind with compassion rather than criticism. Treating your own mind with benevolence restores the connection to your soul.

You and I both know that to grit our teeth and doggedly "replace a negative thought with a positive one" usually feels phony. That's because we often try to take too grand a leap from a dismal thought to a happy thought, rather than just taking one small step forward. How about choosing a thought that's just a teeny bit better? Then another, and another, and another. Then we have taken *incremental* steps instead of one giant leap from feeling horrible to feeling joyous. Here's a possible progression:

- "This family holiday is going to be a nightmare—Nick and Nora are so disagreeable that they'll ruin it for everyone."

- "I think I'll try complimenting Nora on her cake and watch her smile."

- "I'll seat Nick next to Aunt Mary, and she'll bring out the best in him."

- "The children can do their terrific rendition of 'Jingle Bells.'"

- "We're a family that tries to allow differences in a spirit of love and acceptance."

- "Love is always stronger than despair."

- "This Christmas dinner will be undergirded and surrounded with love."

This is not hocus-pocus, or mere power-of-positive-thinking, nor is it a method of selfish escape from the cares of the world. Rather it's an opening to new revelations, as science and religion walk hand in hand. Though these two world-views have historically been regarded as hostile camps, there is increasing evidence of hallowed common ground.

My first glimpse into this cutting-edge field of study occurred when I was an envelope-stuffing volunteer with the Isthmus Institute in Dallas about twenty years ago. Isthmus was a think-tank in which leaders in the fields of science, medicine, music, and religion regularly exchanged views and searched for common ground. At that time, Dr. Larry Dossey was president of Isthmus, and his persona was one that combined compassion and intellectual rigor. Larry influenced all of us to put aside any fear of new information and to embrace the soul's journey with the mind as well as the heart and body. As he pursued early research in the field, he discovered a number of double-blind studies alerting him to the possibilities of prayer. To him, there was unity in everything, if we would but dig deeply enough, and his insistence on the mysterious power of prayer has broken many barriers of cynicism. I'm grateful to say that his enthusiasm and faith were contagious, spreading to all of us who were fortunate enough to be exposed to his wonderful "disease."

He was a prayer pioneer, devoted to delving into the Mystery of God, no matter where it might lead him. In fact, it led him away from his thriving medical practice in Dallas and into a full-time exploration of the cross-currents of religion and science, resulting in a number of prophetic books, such as *Recovering the Soul, Healing Words* and *Reinventing Medicine,* among others.[11]

Study upon study—from the field of medicine as well as the field of quantum physics—is telling us that the effect of the mind and spirit on the body can be profound. This shouldn't come as any surprise to us. We experience this reality at a very elemental level in our own stress reactions. We hear bad news and our hearts constrict; we are mistreated and feel a lump in our throats; someone unpleasant enters the room and a tension headache forms; we witness something gory and our stomachs do somersaults. The body's innate wisdom, an endowment of the Creator, gives it the ability to respond to our thoughts and emotions, producing very real biochemical consequences. It also alerts us to psychological interactions, a part of the tightly woven matrix of body, mind, and spirit.

So how might our attentiveness to our minds work in practical terms? If, for instance, you become upset with a friend for some real or imagined slight, what would a healthy scenario look like?

- Recognize the negative surge in your body and the onset of obsessive thinking.

- Take a deep breath and acknowledge it: "There's that feeling of rejection beginning again—that terrible not-okay-ness."

- Go to the source of the pain. "This anxiety is coming from my own fear that someone doesn't like me or may be critical of me."

- Recall your history. "I never do seem able to think straight when I get fearful like this."

- Be compassionate toward your own fear and woundedness and wait for it to pass. If you wish, you may breathe a prayer, such as "Breathe on me, breath of God."

Clarity will begin to appear; other angles may present themselves, as you reconnect with reality, thinking:

"She has always treated me well in the past"; or

"We have a long history together"; or

"She must have reasons that are important to her; I need to talk with her about it"; or

"She may have pressures and concerns that I don't know about."

Then, you may be able to move toward thoughts such as: "I choose not to place my self-esteem in the hands of another person"; then, "I will live out of my own container of love and compassion, regardless of others' actions"; then finally "I am connected to God and my own sense of wholeness."

All this is based, of course, on a belief that God's nature is not that of an angry, disappointed parent who's eager to whack us. Like the loving father in the story of the Prodigal Son, God is pained at our own suffering, self-inflicted or otherwise. As we dare to see ourselves through God's loving eyes, wrapping ourselves in compassion, we automatically reach out to enclose others in the same loving embrace.

Science is repeatedly telling us to monitor what we eat, that our physical health is reliably related to our choices. Doesn't it also make sense to be responsible about what our minds ingest? If the force of God, in whose image we are made, provides the strength to push a weed up through the concrete, why do we have trouble acknowledging such power simply because we don't quite understand it?

Despite its conundrums and caveats, this idea of the power of our own minds to influence reality has God's grace and creativity written all over it. Our ability to transform our thoughts is a powerful inward maneuver and holds an essential key to letting go.

For Reflection

1. What creative outlet piques your interest—makes you lose track of time?

2. What messages do you tend to give yourself? What is the level of your negative self-talk? Are your thoughts peppered with shoulds, oughts, and musts?

3. How might you learn the skill of harnessing a negative thought and letting it go?

13
Allowing

Then your light shall break forth like the morning and your healing shall spring forth speedily. (Isa 58:8)

You have made known to me the path of life; you will fill me with joy in your presence . . . (Ps 16:11a)

If we hope for what we do not see, we wait for it with patience. Likewise the Spirit helps us in our weakness; for we do not know how to pray as we ought, but the Spirit intercedes for us with sighs too deep for words. (Rom 8:25–26)

At some point in the journey of letting go, it's time to stop striving. After leaning forward into *awareness, availability*, and *action*, there comes a time to become still, settle back, and *allow* the process to work.

Nature abounds with rich reminders of this patient relinquishment. The caterpillar enters the darkness of the cocoon, staying in the shadowy stillness until the transformation into a butterfly is complete. Once I tried opening a cocoon to "release" the butterfly from its straitjacket. It slowly unfolded in beautiful colors and, though wobbly, it looked ready to try its wings. However, the tempting newness didn't last long. It sputtered, stumbled, and fell over to one side—not yet ready for the freedom of flight.

The same thing occurs in my eagerness to produce new tomato seedlings in the spring. Many times in haste I've transplanted them too soon. I've seized control and tried to make it happen just a little bit too early. On occasion I've even gently pried down into the dirt to check on the tiny roots, trying to be sure that growth was actually taking place. You can imagine the results of that maneuver! Whether in the garden of your home or the garden of your soul, the process is the same. Plant the seeds, tend them lovingly, and *allow* them to grow.

But the metaphor that speaks to me most vividly is one that an emergency room physician suggested. He explained it this way: "Let's say you come into the ER with a gash in your arm that needs stitches. The bleeding, the pain, the very sight of it make you *aware* that you need to seek help. You drive to the hospital to make yourself *available* to healing methods. Then comes the *action phase.* As a physician, I must tend the wound, paying careful attention to cleaning out bacteria, probing it for other areas of injury—even though it may hurt to do it. Then I can sew it up and *allow* God's natural healing process to do its remarkable work. Even the scab itself is evidence of automatic healing taking place. I don't make the mistake of taking out the stitches tomorrow to check and see if it is closing properly. You and I must trust the process and *accept* the scar."

I've heard the story that once Albert Einstein was asked what he thought was the most important question a human being could ask. His surprising reply was, "Is the universe a friendly place?"

When I first heard that anecdote, I thought the answer was too glib and simplistic to take seriously. Then slowly, its profound meaning began to sink in. After reflection, I realized how vitally important it is to be able to answer "yes" to that question, even in the face of catastrophes and injustices. Einstein seemed to be pointing toward a benevolent reliability at the very heart of things.

- That gash in the arm has the capacity to heal itself.

- The sun rises and sets daily, without our intervention.

- Solar energy warms the earth and enlivens the plants.

- Ordinary people make heroic sacrifices for others, with no hope of repayment.

- We feel most connected with the image of God within us when we love.

Implicit in this business of *allowing* is a basic paradigm shift, one from "my work for God" to "God's work *in* me." This is not a grudging acquiescence ("Okay, I'll let go, but I know this probably won't work."). Nor is it a disguised reluctance ("Of course, I *want* to let it go, but it's entrenched too deeply; the loss was too painful for me to let it go."). Remember, letting go is not condoning or ignoring, not erasing the loss or pretending it never happened. It is acknowledging the feelings, admitting that it is hard, but choosing to do it anyway. You want to be free of the burden, whatever it is.

Once again, Sue Monk Kidd found just the right words to describe this dismantling process:

> First, there is the active work we do with the conscious, surface attachments in our life—those patterns we recognize and can campaign against. . . .
> By our own sweat and effort we work to let go. . . . Having done all we can, we allow God to work directly on the more secret and deeply ingrained

attachments. . . . We allow God to release us through the experiences, encounters, and events that come to us.[1]

How can we aid this necessary movement from active to passive? What spiritual tools can put us in the posture of *allowing*? What can remind us to take our hands off the wheel and let go? See if any of the following suggestions seem plausible for you.

Body Prayers

> For your steadfast love is before my eyes, and I walk in faithfulness to you.
> (Ps 26:3)

To speak about the obvious interaction between body, mind, and spirit has become so commonplace that we dismiss it as a cliché—oh, yeah, *that again.* But if we're indeed created in this remarkable network, it seems reasonable to engage *all* parts of ourselves in the letting-go process. After all, transformation comes *through* the body, not away from it or in spite of it.

Consider the differences you feel when praying in a variety of body positions—standing, sitting, walking, kneeling, eyes open, eyes closed. The very nature of the prayer seems altered by what the body brings to it. What practices might give the body an opportunity to enhance our prayer of release?

Parable Walk

Engage the power of your body through taking a parable walk. Allow God to speak to you through a spiderweb, through the shape of a tree, through the sound of the wind, through a raindrop. Be open to a personal parable as you stop and look at whatever seems to capture your attention.

A woman I met on a retreat once described a powerful experience of letting go as she opened herself to the divine Presence one beautiful autumn day. Leaves of every shape and color were fluttering around her, and they seemed to be calling for her attention. Her pace slowed as she reached down to pick them up for a closer look.

There was a large red leaf with brown around the edges, reminding her of her red hot rage against her mother-in-law and how it "scorched" the edges of her family life; she let it fall to the ground.

There was a small leaf with dozens of busy little lines, visually reminding her of a persistent tendency to be a busybody, engaging in small, petty gossip; she released it and kept on walking.

There was a magnificent yellow leaf, absolutely perfect in color and symmetry, as yet untouched by autumn dryness. In it she saw her façade of perfection. The act of tossing it into the lake strengthened her intention to let go.

Sometimes just the feel of the wind in your face can be a tactile reminder of the *ruach* of God, the breath of life itself. Put on your walking shoes, open your heart to releasing your resistance, and take a *step* toward freedom.

Labyrinth

> Stand at the crossroads, and look, and ask for the ancient paths, where the good way lies; and walk in it, and find rest for your souls. (Jer 6:16)

Stella remarked suspiciously, "Walking around in circles seems to me a weird way to pray!" The mysterious contours of the labyrinth confound some folks and inspire others. This ancient "sacred geometry" has served as a meditative tool for hundreds of years and is a powerful symbol of wholeness. It represents for many the spiral nature of the spiritual journey inward into one's soul, then out again into the world—truly a pathway with a purpose. No wonder this image is enjoying such a renaissance these past few years. It offers tranquility to the mind, serenity to the spirit, and engages the body as an instrument of letting go.

Here are some suggestions for framing your labyrinth prayer. Pause at the entrance, praying that God will lead you inside your deepest self to discover those things that need releasing. When you reach the center, spend some time in each of the center "petals" if possible, allowing God to bring forth that which you might consider letting go—distractions, cares, worries, attachments. In a time of prayer, leave those things in the center. Follow the path back out again, unburdened by anything that might impede your steps toward loving service to God and others.

Dance

I remember the day Tilden Edwards introduced the possibility of dancing prayer to our class at the Shalem Institute. Our group of twenty-six adults was as scared and skittish as a group of first-graders. Through the Institute's two-year training program in spiritual guidance, we had been exposed to many meaningful spiritual disciplines—from icons to meditative practice to praying the Bible—but this one was clearly outside our comfort zone. In his generous and gracious way, our leader explained the traditions and potential of engaging the body in prayer, giving those who felt massive resistance permission to excuse themselves from the practice, if they wished. Several quietly left the room.

Those of us who stayed were invited to spend some time in silence, allowing our bodies to move freely to the music in any way that felt authentic to us as an expression of our prayer. The lights were dimmed, and restful, melodic music filled the room. After quite some time, one person got up, then another and another, each moving independently and prayerfully. I think each of us tried to avoid eye contact and to create a feeling of complete safety and acceptance. It was probably the most challenging of any of the disciplines we attempted, but one that *embodied* the relinquishment and abandonment to God that we were seeking.

I became keenly aware of the enormous barrier most of us live with—that of timidity and embarrassment about our bodies. This awkwardness causes a host of unspoken questions to bubble up: "What will everyone think?" "Can I let go in my body as well as in my spirit?" "Can the body *teach* my heart how to do this?" Needless to say, we learned a visceral lesson in letting go as we haltingly danced our private prayer of release.

Breathwork

> We must be able to let go and be carried by the downdrafts and updrafts of the breath of God. —Margaret Guenther[2]

"I wish I had more *time* to devote to my spiritual life." The answer to this frequent lament is usually not so much a matter of time as it is a broadening of our prayer boundaries. Let's remember that we have one prayer tool that is with us every day, all the time—regular as clockwork—our very own breath. Why not use this natural apparatus as a focal point in our journey toward the sacred?

Even language itself points us in this direction. The root words of "spirit" and "soul" relate to breath in many ancient languages, including Greek, Latin, and Hebrew. Our ancestors are trying to tell us something vital about what it means to be truly alive. Focusing on our breath—literally the life within us—brings us squarely into the present moment, drawing our energy back to the center, pulling our projections from the past and future. We can join the apostle Paul in his affirmation in Gal 2:20, ". . . it is no longer I who live, but it is Christ who lives in me."

Every single exhalation is a physical expression of letting go. Allow it to be the carrier of whatever might need to be released in your life. You might even formulate a prayer that rides the crest of your breath, such as, "God of Freedom," (on inhale), "I let this go" (on exhale); or "Lord of Healing, transform this thought."

My friend Teresa was under a doctor's care for persistent and painful digestive distress. The familiar syndrome of more medication, more side effects, more stress had left her exhausted and edgy. In fact, she was downright *angry* that this condition was interrupting her busy, productive life.

"I've got to change the way I'm looking at this," she said thoughtfully. "Instead of being so mad at this thing, I'd better start *listening* to it." And she did.

A very imaginative, spirited person, Teresa even decided to give the discomfort a name. She called it "Sophie." She began to speak to Sophie as well as to listen to her. She noticed that one of the precursors to the pain was shallow, rapid breathing. When the discomfort began, she would take a deep breath, envisioning the Holy Spirit, the breath of God, entering her. Her exhale was a breathing out of anxiety and pain. Then she would playfully say to herself, "Okay, Sophie . . . I hear you. What are you trying to tell me?"

And the messages were not surprising. She noticed the pain mounting every time she crammed too much stuff into one day, even if it was good stuff. She noticed her stomach tighten every time she pushed a deadline, every time she felt that the fate of the world was resting on her shoulders. As a minister, she was often swamped with hospital visits and fretted constantly about not being able to give adequate time to this part of her work. Again she employed her breath, visualizing the breath of God enlivening her, then exhaling that loving energy into the world.

She replaced some of the fretting with wise decisions. Frequently, she called hospitalized patients and chatted over the phone, saying, "Mrs. Jones, I can't get there in person today, but I wanted you to know I'm praying for you and will be by to see you soon. Tell me how you're doing."

Teresa began to lighten up, to realize her limitations, and to stop taking herself so seriously. Increasingly, she engages her breath as an intake of God's wisdom and spirit.

"My breath reminds me that I'm not alone," she said with a smile. "It isn't all up to me. I feel a sense of the Holy Spirit as a helpful companion."

As for "Sophie," Teresa now regards her former arch-enemy as a wise and trusted friend who cares enough to demand her attention.

Exercise

Fran was a runner, still clad in her warm-up suit and sport shoes when she arrived at my house for a spiritual direction session. Young, sleek, extremely intelligent, she brought the same vibrant energy to her spiritual life as she invested in her physical and academic lives. Reared in a very conservative church with a tradition of strictly verbal prayer, her spirit seemed ready to burst out of its constrictive container that morning, like a runner poised at the starting line.

"It seems I don't know how to pray anymore," she complained. "I lose interest quickly; it feels empty and lifeless." God as a King—separate and "out there"—while she, the servant, remained way "down here," was losing reality for her. The Spirit was inviting her to expand her notion of who and what God is.

The conversation (as well as the energy) shifted as she began to talk about her morning run. "Gosh, it was great this morning," she began. "The sky was blue, the wind was in my face, the leaves and flowers were a zillion colors—I just felt so *alive!*" All of a sudden, the unexpected words came out of my mouth, "Fran, your body was *praying!*" From that moment on, her running and her praying became intertwined. She intentionally dedicated her morning runs to conversation with God, a time that was deeply enriched by the participation of her body. She envisioned herself as breaking free, letting go of all that was keeping her from a full experience of God.

Not only walking and running, but also yoga, t'ai chi, qi gong, and a host of other exercise modalities lend themselves to body prayer. Look for ways to use your exercise routine as a spiritual tool. Your body can be a valuable ally in your quest for freedom as it carries your intention to release whatever barriers may be standing in your way.

Imagination

From counting sheep to envisioning a business plan, our imaginations connect us daily to the world of possibility. Robert was a man in the throes of a collapsing world—a troubled marriage, a dead-end job, precarious health. He was visited regularly by the all-too-familiar "night terrors," where he couldn't decide what to worry about first. His pleading prayers seemed of little comfort at 3 AM—that is, until he hit on an image that clicked in his psyche and provided a pathway to rest. He imagined himself the lone passenger in a beautiful hot air balloon that was ready to leave the ground. He is eager to soar, but the balloon won't budge. He looks down to see that sandbags are attached all around the balloon base, weighing it down and prohibiting its flight. One by one, he names each sandbag and cuts the line, feeling lighter with each release. As his feeling of buoyancy increases, he is usually able to drift back to sleep as the imaginary balloon carries him aloft. . . .

Once I heard teacher Flora Wuellner talk about her concept of a "*soaking prayer.*" She recalled occasions where fatigue, burnout, or despair made it impossible to pray in her usual manner. "Then," she explained with a smile, "I run a tub full of hot water, pour in some sweet-smelling oil, and just *soak up* the comfort of God. I feel completely enclosed in love as I allow the Spirit to pray *for* me as I release my concerns."

When the imagination connects with truth at a visceral, bodily level, something *clicks* within us. This happened for me when I read Father Thomas Green's descriptive metaphor for the process of allowing. In his insightful book, *When the Well Runs Dry*, he called it *floating*. Think about your first efforts at floating. Didn't you try to keep your head out of the water? Weren't you rigid at first, afraid to trust the water to hold you up? Floating, says Green, is difficult not because it demands much skill but because it demands much letting go. The secret of floating is in learning not to do all the things we instinctively want to do. If we try to make it happen through our own efforts, we are soon exhausted and find ourselves sinking. We must learn to be at home in the sea that is God, "with no visible means of support except the water whose ebb and flow, whose sudden surgings, we cannot predict or control." Green adds:

> The swimmer is intensely active and is going someplace; the floater yields to the flow of the water and savors fully being where he is. He, too, is going someplace, but that is the concern of the current which carries him. His major decision is whether to trust the tide. If he does not, he must guide himself by his swimming strokes; if he does, he can relax and surrender himself totally to the tide, and live fully the present moment. The problem is that we must decide whether we want to swim or to float.[3]

Some of us float pretty well in familiar waters, but when we drift beyond the safety zone, we frantically flail our arms in an effort to swim back to safety.

God wants us to trust enough to float in confidence and freedom of spirit—*allowing* the sea that is God to support us.

Sacraments and Services
Laurie was going down the aisle to receive the Eucharist, her mind still reviewing all the hateful words. There had been so much conflict in her church that she couldn't imagine how the fences could ever be mended. Accusations, misunderstandings, whispers, gossip, taking sides—all of it engulfed her as she approached the altar. She recalled the gospel reading that morning—the story about the disciples being told to "shake off the dust from your feet as you leave" (Matt 10:14). Could she do that? Could she shake off the hostilities, let them go, and surrender them at the altar?

In her prayer, she offered that thought as sincerely as she could as she slowly knelt, imagining the dust falling gently from the soles of her shoes. As she returned to her seat, she focused of the feeling of her feet coming in contact with the floor, unencumbered with the dust of distress.

As we go about our liturgical lives, as we find ourselves in worship settings of various kinds, why not use them as tools in our letting go process? The next time you kneel for communion, imagine yourself "shaking the dust from your feet," arising with Christ at your side to lead you away from the bondage that is keeping you spiritually chained.

The season of Advent holds great potential for expressions of letting go. You may choose to identify with Mary and see yourself as pregnant with new life. Ask prayerfully what newness God may be inviting you to. Use the four-week period of expectancy to incubate the changes and then celebrate the new life God has instilled within you.

Quite a number of churches are scheduling regular healing services. Find one in your community and let it be a symbol of your commitment to let go. As you are marked with the sign of the cross in oil on your forehead, allow that to be a symbol of your commitment. When the grasping attachment inevitably creeps back in, remind yourself that you are "marked with the sign of the cross—the ultimate symbol of letting go."

Even weddings and funerals can carry our commitments. As you celebrate a couple's new life, remind yourself of the scriptural words, "See, I am making all things new" (Rev 21:5). Let it symbolize your new resolve to be uncluttered by any barriers to a life of love.

Funerals bring us face to face with the ultimate letting go—that of our own lives. As we contemplate the foundation of faith that sustains us in those moments, we can use the words of the service to remind us to put things in perspective. If my life were nearing an end, what would be important to me? What hurts and resentments would I need to relinquish? Whose forgiveness might I need to ask? What needs to be gone from my life?

Baptisms are about new beginnings. Each baptismal service provides an opportunity to renew your own baptism, to think about what it means to start over, to be washed in God's grace, to be cleansed of attitudes and habits that keep you from God's best in your life. Imagine that you're literally being washed by waters from heaven, clearing away all that needs to be relinquished. Allow the liturgy of hope and promise to carry you to fresh resolve.

Nature

> To see a world in a grain of sand and a heaven in a wildflower, hold infinity in the palm of your hand and eternity in an hour. —William Blake [4]

> Earth's crammed with heaven, and every bush aflame with the glory of God. —Elizabeth Barrett Browning[5]

Nothing has the potential to move us off dead center quite as powerfully as unexpected encounters in nature. From the meadows to the mountaintops, from the devoted pet to the flight of the bumblebee—the ways that nature nurtures us bring tears to our eyes and resolve to our hearts. And we are often brought into the place of *allowing* the spirit to finally get through to us. The possibilities are endless—the motion of the tides, the cleansing of a rainstorm, the dormancy of winter—all remind us that a force greater than ourselves turns the clock of this universe. Nature immerses us in that power.

Even the lowly snake can show us something about letting go, as nature instills it with a willingness to release the old skin so that a new one can emerge. Never mind that snakes have always been given a bad rap. They may seem slimy and sinister, but my son Harrison, a true snake lover, has taught me through the years that they are neither. Their scales can be incredibly beautiful and intricate, they are most often nonvenomous, and their skin-shedding habits are ready-made images of relinquishment that we can mirror. Obviously, we don't accomplish much in this lifetime if our spirituality is the same at age fifty as it is at age ten. It is frequently necessary to shed old habits, opinions, ideas, attitudes. Like the snake, newness emerges as we shed the old. Many wise teachers of letting go point out the behaviors in the animal kingdom as prime examples of the natural ability to let go and live in the present moment.

Even so, I never imagined that a *plant* could be my teacher. The Spirit seems to be much more willing to speak than we are to listen and surrounds us daily with potent messages.

I had been in desert country for three weeks, alone—not roughing it, for sure, thanks to a friend who had loaned me her house in Scottsdale, but truly and positively alone. *Plenty of time to work out all my issues, listen to God, get some clarity and answers,* I thought. But here I was packing for departure and wondering if anything had really been settled.

I had enjoyed the adventure of being in a strange place, the hikes in the desert, the feeling of independence and competence, but I couldn't say that my questions of relationship and vocation were answered. Still, somehow I hoped the time hadn't been wasted. It had been a unique experience for a middle-aged woman.

As I placed the clothes neatly in the suitcase, I began to feel an overwhelming urge, as if an inner voice were demanding my attention. "Return to Squaw Peak," kept entering my mind. *Why Squaw Peak?* I thought. It wasn't a place I wanted to return to—too crowded, too hot, totally uninspiring. *I must really be losing it,* I thought. But some urgency made me stop in the midst of packing, get in the car, and drive the half-hour to the park.

Surprisingly, I found it almost deserted, so I headed to a trail at the back of the park that I hadn't tried before. For the next hour, I encountered not one single person to distract me. My only companions were the hundreds of saguaro cacti that dotted the Sonoran Desert. As I rounded a bend in the path, I was suddenly face-to-face with an old beaten-up cactus about fifty feet tall. Up close and personal, these stately plants are anything but beautiful. This one sported ragged holes where birds had nested, ugly gashes cut by years of weather and wear. Suddenly I burst into tears. My silent thoughts said clearly, "Look how tall she stands. See how proudly she wears her scars? She is unashamed." I thought of the poignant words I heard from a wise teacher—that God does not look for our degrees or diplomas, but for our scars.

As I gathered my emotions, the gentle inner voice directed me again: "Go to the large boulder over there, sit on it and turn around." As I did, I faced the open desert, dotted with hundreds of saguaro cactus plants, looking like fingers pointing to the sky. After a long silence, the voice urged, "Just be a 'pointer'—I have scores of them. You don't have to be the smartest, the prettiest, the best-educated, or the most engaging. Just be one. Just point up."

I continued to amble along the trail, second-guessing myself. *I must have been out in the desert sun too long. Better hike back to the parking lot and go home.* But after a few moments, I again felt the prompting to turn and sit on a boulder. Astoundingly, I found myself face-to-face with the same cactus over which I had cried, this time approaching her from a different angle. The gigantic plant was situated in the center of a very small rise, surrounded by smaller cacti and desert plants. The thought emerged, "Just be a pointer in your small area of influence; don't try to do everything; just point the way ahead to those on your little hill." And then the most surprising suggestion of all arose: "*Allow people to build nests in your wounds.*"

I was stunned, confused, full of doubts. Of course, by the time I had returned to my car, I had resumed my inner critique, chastising myself for having such a vivid imagination. Time passed, but the experience didn't. As the days turned into weeks and years, not a single feeling, word, or impulse has been dimmed by time. Often when I look at the picture of the saguaro cactus on my desk, I weep for her; I remember her pain and vulnerability; but most of all, I remember her purpose—to stand tall in the dry, desolate landscapes of life and *allow* people to build nests in her wounds. I'm only beginning to realize what her example means for me. In ways I cannot explain, sharing my own scars with others has *allowed* my life to be healed. Nature can be a sacred guide in our process of growth.

For Reflection

1. What is your relationship with your body? How does your body register stress? In what ways does your body participate in your prayer?

2. Compose your own breath prayer. Base its content on your answer to the question: What is your deepest need? Pray it often for a few weeks, attaching it to your breath, inhaling and exhaling. Allow God to inspire your prayer.

3. What nature setting seems to have a calming effect on you? Have you experienced any moments when you felt God's presence? How might you revise your schedule to permit more time in a natural environment—even if it's just a solitary walk in the park?

14
Acceptance

Now the Lord is the Spirit, and where the Spirit of the Lord is, there is freedom. (2 Cor 3:17)

But I have calmed and quieted my soul, like a weaned child with its mother. (Ps 131:2)

One day I was meditating on this simple verse from Psalm 131. Why did the psalmist designate a *weaned* child? Why not an adoring child, a happy child, an obedient child? As I sank into the image, I realized that the weaned child is not asking for anything, not needing anything, not demanding anything—just *accepting what is*. Satisfied. Content in the loving arms of the mother.

This kind of serenity is neither placid nor passive. It exists as a sort of *baseline* to life—a peace that passes all understanding, a feeling of rest in a sea of unrest. Circumstances lived on top of this peace may be chaotic, tragic, exciting, dull, euphoric, happy, sad. But there is a foundation of meaning—a base that undergirds everything with a dependable sort of sacred weight.

Obviously, it seems elusive to us most of the time. Eric Kolbell, in his distinctly beautiful prose, explained it this way in *What Jesus Meant*: "Peace is serenity: it is that inner place we tiptoe to every so often where there is nothing we must change in the present, regret in the past, or dread in the future. It is not necessarily a state of perfection, but it *is* a perfect acceptance of our life as it is being lived at that moment."[1]

Once in a while, a metaphor comes along that clicks our confused spirits into place. During a study of the writings of St. Teresa of Avila, I encountered what is probably the most famous metaphor for the spiritual life in Christian history, and my "truth bell" rang with clarity. In Teresa's *Autogiography*[2], this inspired sixteenth-century Spanish nun devotes a dozen chapters to explaining the stages of a life of prayer. Thomas Green has a briefer, but detailed, discussion of it in *When the Well Runs Dry*.[3] Though the original concept is Teresa's, many seekers through the centuries have made it their own, expressing it in their own terms and experience.

Through the lens of my own life, here's what it came to mean to me. When you begin to pay attention to the spiritual life, it's as if God has planted a garden, and you're trying to figure out how to water it, tend it, make it grow. The experiential stages seem loosely to follow this outline:

- Hauling water. At first, it feels as if you're dipping a heavy wooden bucket in the well, hauling the water to the garden, bucket by bucket.

- Pumping water. Next, you discover a water wheel nearby and you continue to water, but now with a little assistance.

- Stream. Then you notice a stream flowing through the garden, perhaps providing an irrigation system—if you open the gates, it will flow in.

- But in the final stage, you merely *stand in the rain*, accepting the gifts of grace as they wash over you.

When I first imagined myself standing in the rain, I could feel the relief wash over me in a state of effortless joy. Was it really possible to live like that? To continue to till and tend the garden, but to honestly depend on a greater love to shower me like rain soaking my upturned face? Just as each stage of the spiritual life involves less and less effort on our part, the journey of letting go involves a similar dynamic. It moves through *awareness, availability, action, allowing*, and ends in *acceptance*—certainly a kind of "standing in the rain." What practices can help us move toward this place of peace?

Forgiveness

> Bear with one another and, if anyone has a complaint against another, forgive each other; just as the Lord has forgiven you, so you also must forgive. Above all, clothe yourselves with love, which binds everything together in perfect harmony. And let the peace of Christ rule in your hearts. . . . (Col 3:13–15)

We've already made the case for the spiritual and physical benefits of forgiveness. Forgiveness frees the forgiver from the unspeakable burden of entanglement in someone else's nightmare. All great wisdom traditions have singled out forgiveness as a preparation for death itself. Our need to forgive and be forgiven, to "clean the slate," leads us to the peace of *acceptance*.

But there is a vital prerequisite. The process starts with accepting forgiveness for ourselves—really and truly feeling forgiven by God—and forgiveness to ourselves. It was years before I realized the depth of meaning in the simple plea found in the Lord's Prayer: "Forgive us our trespasses as we forgive those who trespass against us." It doesn't say *when*; it says *as*. It is all of a piece, all a part of the same fluid motion. *In some mysterious way, the degree to which we accept the forgiveness of God is the degree to which we are able to forgive others.* It is a concept that is difficult to pin down, to draw a picture of. We're much more accustomed to pointing the finger at ourselves, imagining the righteous judgment of God. Then that same righteous judgment moves from us toward others.

True, we've all done some pretty rotten things, often from ignorance, but sometimes just to make ourselves look better, subtly manipulating others into behaviors that would reflect well on us. And what parent among us doesn't weep in regret for a whole range of shortcomings in rearing our children? Usually, we tend to whitewash and justify our actions, but part of the process of forgiving others is facing the need of forgiveness ourselves.

So the first step is to prayerfully remind yourself that God forgives *you*. Jesus modeled this on the cross, embodying a forgiveness that included even his murderers. Just as this divine forgiveness envelops *us*, so we must accept the fact that God forgives others in the same way. One of the prerequisites of forgiveness is accepting the forgiveness of God toward all of us. Then you merely *join it*.

Now to the nitty-gritty of how to forgive:

1. Feel the pain in your body. Find a safe place, a trusted friend, a wise counselor, and get it out. Tell what happened. Own the feelings. You can't forgive a wound that you don't feel. Stay with this part of the process until you feel emptied of it.

2. Join the current of forgiveness. Pray to join in the flow of forgiveness that belongs to a loving God. You don't have to generate the forgiveness; just join the Love that is greater than your own. Admit that you can't do it under your own steam and trust that it is not all up to you.

3. Swim with the current, not against it. Make concrete plans to move out of the victim mode. How am I telling the story of what happened? Am I repeating it over and over, casting myself as a victim? Try to talk about it less, and when you do, speak from a place of peace, praying for a gentler approach to the problem. Try to move toward ways of talking about it that no longer disturb you. Monitor your behaviors.

4. Release the baggage into God's hands. You choose to carry the burden no longer.

5. Create a container for the healing. This amounts to doing your own inner work. This is not an inner space where you go over your list of complaints or prayer petitions about that person, but space where you can meet your own authentic Self and encounter the Spirit within. Remember, at your core, you are made in the image of God. That self, even with its warts, is created with the capacity for love and forgiveness.

Own that, and begin to live out of that bottomless well of compassion that God provides.

I'm convinced that forgiveness can become a way of life. Despite our tendency toward vindictiveness, one-upmanship, and tit-for-tat, there is a power that can enhance our best intentions. At the same time, our resistance dissolves like melting snow and we can *accept* life for what it is.

Gratitude

> . . . give thanks in all circumstances. . . . (1 Thess 5:18)

My favorite definition of gratitude is "the recurrent acknowledgment of what is working; recalling the abundance that exists already." An attitude of gratitude is pure dynamite when it comes to letting go. Gratitude uplifts, excites, transforms, and enables us to *accept* life because it trains us to view life differently.

If we give in to the voices of our culture, we will sink deeper and deeper into paralyzing despair. The steady barrage of murder and mayhem—countless signs of our inhumanity to each other—can erode our optimism and grind our gratitude into dust. Spiritual disciplines of thanksgiving seem to balance the scales of life, reminding us that light and dark exist together, both outside us and inside us. Our intentional focus on gratitude can literally change our view of life, not in a phony Pollyanna way, but in a life-affirming way. It helps us accept the things we cannot change.

These two practices of gratitude can help us let go:

Gratitude Journal

So many people have been credited with the origin of this idea that I don't know whom to thank. It's a deceptively simple procedure.

- Purchase a journal with an interesting, inviting cover, for thanksgiving purposes only.

- Each evening list five things that happened that day for which you are grateful.

(Note: Be specific. No generalities, like "Everyone was nice to me today." Pay attention to the details, such as "I'm grateful for the way the sun felt on the back of my neck while I was weeding the flowerbed; I'm grateful for the hug John gave me as he left for work; I'm grateful for the smell of the baby's skin when I lifted her from her bath; I'm grateful that Mary called me and asked me how my cold was.")

- If your day has been so dismal that there seems to be nothing to list, be creative: "I'm grateful that I made it through this awful day. I'm grateful that I survived that council meeting without punching someone out. I'm grateful for the doctor who was kind enough to stay with me for awhile after he gave me the diagnosis."

This may seem to be an assignment for a first-grader. If you can put aside your resistance and try it for at least one month, you'll begin to see a difference in the way you approach your day. Knowing that you have your evening assignment ahead, you'll begin to pre-program your mind to look for objects of gratitude. In other words, you will start noticing things you've never noticed before—the graces that are woven through your days.

Thanksgiving Diet
This practice employs a different modality to accomplish the same thing. It can be an individual prayer that you employ around mealtimes, allowing the meal to be a reminder of your focus. You can also include your family in this practice, infusing your mealtimes with specific points of thanksgiving:

Breakfast: What graces are getting me ready for this day? (eight hours of sleep, oatmeal, Susie's hug, morning prayer time, new pink shirt) What are the good things I think will happen today?

Lunch: What people or events during the morning have contributed to my well-being? What is one thing I can look forward to this afternoon? (Even if it's only a five-minute nap or a cup of tea.)

Dinner: What was the best moment of my entire day? What was the most challenging? What is at least one new thing for which I'm thankful that I never noticed before?

Daily Examen
This variation of the ancient practice of daily confession, practiced for centuries by religious orders, is my personal favorite. It's re-framed in positive terms and is directed toward the discovery of the life-giving influences in your daily round. People who are puzzled about what "lights their fire" can soon find out after employing this practice for a few weeks.

At the close of the day, answer these questions in your journal:

- What touched or moved me today?

- What surprised me today?

- What inspired me today?

- What was life-giving to me today?

- What felt life-taking to me today?

- What did I learn about God and myself today?

Anxiety to Appreciation
This simple exercise not only helps to release frustration, but also transforms some of our daily irritations into means of grace.

In the following situations, take a deep cleansing breath and turn your eyes and/or thoughts to objects of gratitude.

When stalled in traffic, be grateful for your car and what it means in your life; make it a rolling sanctuary by putting on soothing music and taking deep breaths of appreciation. If you're on a train or a bus, take time to pray for those around you, seeing them as children of God with unique needs and yearnings.

When stopped at an intersection by a train, take time to review your favorite vacation trips. What was the hotel like? The food? The sand and surf? The scenery?

When you're put on hold on the phone, mentally list the people in your life to whom you're happily connected by phone—family members, kids away at college, old friends—and say a prayer of gratitude for the richness they bring to your life and for the technology that makes it possible.

When you're in a check-out line, take a moment to be grateful for the abundance in your life—food, appliances, clothing, gadgets, mountains of stuff that bring joy to your household.

When the computer seems to be taking forever to spit out the information you want, recall the days when it had to all be done by hand—all the records in quadruplicate, the searching through endless file cabinets for the right information, the inevitably lost records. Feel gratitude for this remarkable technology.

You can imagine the effect of these bursts of gratitude. It's a practical way of affirming that your prayers are being answered, even if the world says otherwise. Not only will a thankful attitude facilitate your process of letting go, but the appreciation will melt into *acceptance*.

Symbols

Symbols remind us of what we value. They recall where we've been, what we believe, and what we can become. The flag celebrates our freedom "from sea to shining sea." A wedding ring symbolizes a commitment to a loving relationship. The cross reminds of the sacrificial love of Jesus.

A symbol that we perform with our bodies is called a ritual. When we engage in rituals that commemorate our decisions, we can be moved to a place of deep *acceptance* of that which we are honoring. A personally designed ritual can serve as a deliberate exterior act to signify an interior intention—engaging the whole self in letting go.

Personal Ritual
Eleanor's relationship with her boyfriend Greg was on the rocks. This man to whom she had been engaged for two years had broken things off abruptly, admitting that he had found someone else. Her devastation and anger dominated every waking moment and was on the verge of ruining her health. A

good counselor had helped her work through her feelings of rejection and rage, and she was ready to move on. As a symbol of that decision she created a beautiful ritual to mark the new beginning.

She stood beside a serene lake near her home with a single, long-stemmed rose in her hand. She took a deep breath and conjured up every memory she could about the relationship. As she visualized a life-giving moment, she pulled a red rose petal from the blossom to honor the memory and tossed it gently into the lake. When a painful memory came to mind, she plucked a sharp thorn from the rose stem and dropped it, too, into the water. When the memories, as well as the petals and thorns, were exhausted, she tossed what was left of the rose far out into the lake in a final letting go. Though the ritual didn't erase the pain or deaden the disappointment, it helped her turn the corner in her recovery and come to *accept* the loss.

Charles, a quiet, thoughtful man by nature, was what my grandmother would have called a "worry wart." The more he obsessed about the state of the world, the more despondent he became. Even his life of faith became contaminated by cynicism as he pursued unanswerable questions. Why was that child born blind? What did God require of us anyway? Why did the righteous suffer? Finally he realized the darkness was closing in on him and he needed to divert the dark energy.

Finally he arrived at a concrete ritual to help him deal with the dilemmas that plagued him. He bought a carved wooden box and dubbed it his "Question Box." As he placed it on a nearby shelf in his office, he promised that when he felt himself twisting in the wind of a cosmic question, he would write it on a piece of paper and relegate it to the special container. After months of doing this, he lightened up a bit, telling his friends with a smile, "Oh, that box over there contains all the questions I'm going to ask God when I die!" He was on his way to accepting the unfairness and imperfection of life.

Group Ritual

Group rituals offer the blessing of mutual support and encouragement. Remember the campfire ceremonies of your youth? The experience of writing your "sins" on a piece of paper to be burned in the bonfire? From the imaginative ceremonies of youth to the more sophisticated liturgies of adulthood, we are surrounded by powerful reminders of that which we honor and value.

When congregations celebrate the Lord's Supper, we engage in a deeply moving remembrance of Christ. When ashes are placed on our foreheads each Ash Wednesday, we mark the beginning of the season of Lent. The Advent Candle symbolizes our anticipation of the coming of Jesus. Symbols provide a pathway to meaning to our spiritual lives.

Another historical example of group ritual is the Flower Communion, a part of the Unitarian tradition. The leaders originally established it as a ceremony that would be emotionally satisfying for the diverse congregation from Catholic, Protestant and Jewish backgrounds. Everyone is asked to bring a flower to place in a large vase as they enter the sanctuary. This represents the many unique people who come together to form one church body. During the service the bouquet is brought forward and a prayer is offered to affirm both the unity and the diversity of the group. After the consecration of the flowers, each participant takes a flower other than the one they originally brought, symbolizing mutual respect and the grace brought by their various gifts. What a creative way to affirm the acceptance of diversity and the letting go of barriers.

Sometimes a symbol can "announce itself" unexpectedly, and an ordinary lonely walk on the beach can be transformed into a ritual of acceptance. Such was the case for me one summer afternoon on Georgia's short stretch of Atlantic coastline.

I certainly wasn't looking for a mystical experience. I don't think I was even praying in any sort of conscious sense, but some part of me must have been open. I didn't realize I was about to undergo a major shift in my inner life as the pristine beach stretched out before me—firm, flat, brown sand as far as the eye could see. Grateful to have a free afternoon in the midst of a busy conference week, I had driven the few miles from the retreat center to this familiar vacation spot, the scene of at least twenty family summertimes.

As I meandered along the water's edge, the memories came flooding back—my sons and their friends shrieking in the surf, tumbling in the waves and shouting their boyhood banter. Yes, this beach marked many milestones of my adult life—both the glorious and the tragic. My solitary stroll took me past the shell beds, visible at low tide, and I recalled years of shell-collecting. Our youngest son Harrison—a dedicated beach bum by age four—was the champion shell spotter, always the first to spy a giant shell being washed to shore. With perfect timing, he would splash boldly into the ankle-deep water and grab the shell before the sea could reclaim it. Our bookshelves were filled with prize specimens.

Suddenly, my reverie was interrupted by the sight of a huge shell tumbling on to the shore. Even from a few yards away, I could see the distinctive spiral shape of a channeled whelk and ran quickly to rescue it from the approaching wave. I splashed in—shoes, socks and all—and rescued the shell from the pull of the tide.

But then I took a look at it. The delicate beading on the circular top was camouflaging the rest of the shell—chipped and discolored and flawed beyond repair. Disappointed at its condition, I drew my arm back to toss it into the water, but something inside stopped me. Involuntary tears began to pour down my cheeks as I clutched the battered shell to my chest, my heart breaking for her brokenness. Just like the saguaro cactus, I was feeling a strange kinship with what I considered an inanimate object.

We were soul sisters. She and I had been through some stormy times on that stretch of beach, leaving us both with scars and barnacles. Then I discovered another striking similarity that took my breath away. Beneath the chipped exterior of the shell, an interior world had become visible—a strong center—a straight solid structure in the center that held it all together, and miraculously, it was unbroken and perfect. My life flashed before me as I relived the sorrow, loss, and humiliation. The seashell's story became my own, and the remainder of the walk became a ritual of *acceptance*.

I smiled as I remembered all those perfect shells on the bookshelf, reflecting my own preoccupation with perfection. No chips, no flaws—just a polished exterior life. And I knew that the precious shell in my hand, whose outside was scarred by life's buffeting, would be placed at the center of the collection. It would be my symbol of the ultimate beauty of brokenness.

Pain subsides as it is infused with meaning and purpose. Acceptance compels us to say, "This is how it is; I can't change it. I'm tired of talking about how awful it was. I accept the fact that this happened to me, and I'm okay."

Sue Monk Kidd shares a journal entry in *When the Heart Waits*, reflecting on the subject of acceptance:

> Accept life—the places it bleeds and the places it smiles. That's your most holy and human task. Gather up the pain and the questions and hold them like a child upon your lap. Have faith in God, in the movement of your soul. Accept what *is*. Accept the dark. It's okay. Just be true. You're loved. Your pain is God's pain. Go ahead and embrace the struggle and chaos of it all, the splendor, the messiness, the wonder, the agony, the joy, the conflict. Love all of it. Remember that little flame on the Easter candle. Cup your heart around it. Your darkness will become the light.[4]

For Reflection

1. Think of one person for whom you harbor resentment. Imagine how it might feel to be free of that negative energy inside you. What are you gaining from holding on to the feelings?

2. What steps might you take specifically to enhance your feelings of gratitude?

   Perhaps you might write five letters to people who have made a difference in your life, telling them how grateful you are for them.

3. Think of a situation in your life that has been difficult for you to accept. Devise a ritual to symbolize your intention to let it go.

Part IV
Am I on the Right Track?

Litmus Tests of Letting Go

Pleasure is always derived from something outside you, whereas joy arises from within. —Eckhart Tolle[1]

Compassion was the litmus test for the prophets of Israel, for the rabbis of the Talmud, for Jesus, for Paul, and for Muhammad, not to mention Confucius, Lai-tsu, the Buddha, or the sages of the Upanishads.

—Karen Armstrong[2]

You will know them by their fruits. (Matt 7:16)

. . . the fruit of the Spirit is love, joy, peace, patience, kindness, generosity, faithfulness, gentleness, and self-control. (Gal 5:22, 23a)

This is not a final exam. This is not a checklist to see if you're passing muster in Letting Go 101. However, it is a kind of behavioral barometer that provides a loose measure of how you're doing. As an interested observer of this process, I've noticed some recurrent signposts along the path among people who are sincerely committed to relinquishing their barriers to growth. They tend to exhibit certain characteristics—slowly, but surely, like plants in a well-tended garden.

This doesn't happen in a flash, of course. Nor does it happen completely. In fact, if you totally embody all the attitudes I'm about to mention, you would be a candidate for sainthood. So I offer them merely as unofficial signals that grace the lives of those who are learning the art of letting go.

I began compiling this random list of attributes following an interesting conversation with a long-time spiritual direction client. For many months, Patricia had been knocking on the door of release, but couldn't quite enter the room. There was resistance that was well justified and firmly entrenched. She had been understandably hesitant to release the reasons for holding on—the yes-buts—after all, they were very real. But continuing to re-visit them in our spiritual direction sessions had stalled her in a familiar, "stuck" place. The recurrent resistance was being steadily worn down by grace and by her own persistent commitment.

Bit by stubborn bit, she had been chipping away at her behavioral blocks, looking them straight in the face and courageously calling them by name. And it wasn't easy work. Her barriers were wolves in sheep's clothing—things our society would view as good traits—such as a dogged determination to succeed, a vigorous work ethic, commitment to a meaningful cause, and a sense of super-responsibility. These attributes formed the core of her self-esteem, and she was proud of it. Then the shadow sides of those traits began to take their toll. Perfectionism, continual self-criticism, and feelings of competitiveness were making her anxious and stressed out. Her body got into a reactive mode, demanding medical attention. And that got *her* attention.

Tracking the trail of causes took some time. Stress-producers lurked around every corner. She admitted that scaling the height of her profession was now out of her reach, yet she couldn't let go of the feelings of disappointment. Deeply committed to her ministry and calling, she was often embroiled in the inevitable conflicts and demands of church life, evoking yet more stress. Even in the face of increasing encroachments on her personal time, she still drove herself relentlessly, trying to get it all done.

But Patricia continued to believe that God would lead her to wholeness, if she would do her part faithfully. She began to confront her barriers in earnest, slowly relinquishing her defensiveness about the *reasons* for her condition. Though an energetic extrovert, she embarked on the practice of centering prayer in an effort to release control in the silence of God. I knew the weeks of daily practice had been very difficult for her, but she continued to trust God even when she detected no results whatsoever. She made a point of noticing her persistent negative thoughts and behaviors, owning and releasing, owning and releasing. And she kept showing up for her monthly spiritual direction appointment, no matter how busy she was, willing to monitor her deepening relationship with God.

"So, how are things going?" I asked casually as we began our time together. "Is that situation with your colleague still tense? Are you still friends?" (I recalled that months before she had been highly anxious about a particular relationship, still harboring some resentments and wounded feelings.)

"Oh, I don't worry about that much anymore, I guess," she replied offhandedly. "She has a right to her feelings. It's not really about me, anyway; actually, it doesn't feel personal. I just want to love and accept her and our friendship as it is, not as it was."

I leaned forward and smiled. "Did you just hear yourself?"

"What do you mean?" she asked.

"You're letting go without even realizing it," I said eagerly.

Once again I noticed that one of the characteristics of *process* is that its results tend to sneak up on us—to appear as serendipity, not as the outcome of conscious striving. Patricia had become *aware* of her need to let go; she had made herself *available* to all sorts of helpful input; she had acted out in her experience what she was learning in her head; she had *allowed* God's healing to work—unseen and unevaluated; then she had *accepted* the situation as it was.

"Is this how I know I'm on the right track?" Patricia inquired. "I felt as if I wasn't getting anywhere, but maybe I am, after all! What are some other signs of progress?"

So I began to ponder her question. I thought about the demeanor and habits of people I knew who seemed most authentically themselves in the best sense of the word, those who exuded safety and acceptance to those around them, those who seemed to have let go of impediments to love of God, self, and others. Not surprisingly, the same traits and tendencies kept showing up.

Letting go isn't a matter of clicking off one switch and flipping on another. Rather it's a gradual, subtle process where certain attitudes seem to emerge over time as one continues toward freedom of spirit. These attributes cut across lines of gender, age, personality type, and religious affiliation. It's as if God is patiently waiting to grow the fruits of the spirit in us, if we will just release what is blocking the flow of grace.

"You will know them by their fruits," Scripture reminds us. Many of us can talk a good game. We can recite the creeds, state unequivocally what we believe (and, by extension, what any "good Christian" ought to believe), and perform worthy works. However, the integration of true growth means that our external acts are the embodiment of what is inside us; there is congruence between inner and outer—no gap between who we are inside and what we project outside—authentic wholeness.

What follows is a partial list of signposts—reliable indications that healing is taking place. Try to resist evaluating them as "all or nothing." The question is not, "Have I perfected these qualities, every day in every way?" Rather, ask yourself, "Do I seem to be moving in this direction—just a little more this month than last month? Do I see signs of subtle change in my thoughts and responses?"

Signposts

- *Less worry.* The differences between responsible concern and needless fretting will become clearer. You will begin to see worry as something that usurps your energy and serves no useful purpose. Fear will lose its motivating force and will produce fewer fear-based reactions.

- *Less striving.* This means more patience with everything—from waiting in traffic to waiting on your own life to unfold. To return to St. Teresa's metaphor, you will experience less hauling water in buckets and more standing in the rain! Striving to make things happen will slowly give way to allowing things to happen with active participation, but without manipulation or control on your part.

- *Less judgment.* You may become less interested in interpreting or directing the actions of others, allowing them to be responsible for their own lives. You will give others the benefit of the doubt, giving them the same acceptance that you desire for yourself.

- *Less guilt.* You will become more sensitive to the difference between meaningful guilt (a failure to be true to your best self that invites change) and senseless guilt (a feeling of inadequacy based on the opinions and expectations of others). The words *ought, should, must,* and *supposed to* will virtually disappear from your vocabulary—replaced by *I will, I choose,* and *I want.*

- *Less self-consciousness.* There will be fewer and fewer internal questions such as: How should I behave? What image do I wish to present? How am I coming across? You will be more comfortable in your own skin. In stressful situations, you will not always assume that you did something wrong or said something offensive. You will cease to take things personally.

- *More response-ability.* There will be a growing awareness that you have a choice in how you respond in any situation. There may be a time-delay in knee-jerk reactions to things that used to set you off, for you will no longer be at the mercy of volatile emotions. You will become increasingly able to *respond rather than react.*

- *More soul-connection, less ego-connection.* This means you are becoming more independent of criticism as well as flattery. The opinions of others may delight, instruct, or disappoint you, but they won't tell you who you are.

- *More cooperation.* You will have a greater capacity to give others accolades, allow them to be in the limelight. Feelings of competition will tend increasingly toward cooperation.

- *More ego-transcendence.* Your capacity to feel pleasure in the pleasure of others will grow, as well as a capacity for concern about events not directly related to your self-interest. You will be willing to invest yourself in tomorrow's world, even thought you may not be around to see it.

- *More appreciation of beauty.* From sunsets to symphonies, beauty in sight and sound will delight and inspire you, giving you a sense of connection with all of life.

- *More comfort with Mystery.* Paradox, uncertainty, and ambivalence will cease to feel like enemies. Your anxiety will be replaced with awe.

- *More connection to body*. You will begin to appreciate your body as a wondrous, multi-faceted creation of God, one through which God guides you. You will learn to identify feelings of resonance (consolation) and resistance (desolation) as internal messages.

- *More acceptance of self and others*. As you are able to truly receive the unconditional love of God, you will accept yourself as okay—warts and all. You will make fewer self-deprecating statements about yourself. By extension, you will have an increased capacity to accept others as they are, even if you don't approve of what they do. You will value diversity, for it will no longer threaten you.

- *More simplicity*. You will find as much delight in a bright red geranium as in a bright red sports car. Too much "stuff" in your life may begin to weigh you down, as you become more aware of the difference between permanent values and transitory values.

- *More ability to live in the moment*. You will act more spontaneously, be more attentive and present to others, and feel less scattered and out of focus.

- *More forgiving attitude*. You will feel increasingly imprisoned by unforgiveness and resentment, as you become more sensitive to their toxic qualities. You will understand that you can forgive people without condoning behavior.

- *More aliveness*. You will feel both pain and pleasure more vividly. Since the Spirit does not give protection from sorrow, you may feel it more keenly than before, yet with more peace.

- *More creativity*. Creative energy will expand and show itself in unexpected ways, not just as paint on a canvas, but as fresh business ideas, lively ways to entertain the grandchildren, new ways to make ordinary moments into extraordinary ones.

- *More gratitude*. Gratitude will grow to be a lens through which you view life, rather than a list of blessings.

- *More capacity to listen*. You can be totally present to others without trying to fix them. You can develop your capacity to listen to God as well.

- *More generosity*. You may want to give with no strings attached, without control or recognition. It will emerge from a deep desire to share.

- *More kindness*. Your actions will come from a reservoir of goodwill. You will be less dependent on how others receive your kindness or how they respond to it. You will sense the difference between pity and true kindness. It will become less what you do and more who you are.

● *More compassion.* You won't simply feel sorry for people; you will share their suffering in a visceral way. Your desire to be of service will come from not from a feeling of guilt, but from a genuine need to share the love of God. This may lead you to put "legs" on your compassion by a growing interest in justice issues. You will act from choice rather than duty.

● *More trust.* There will be a growing confidence in a benevolent universe created by a loving God, a blessed assurance that you are never abandoned, that the Spirit cares for you. You will trust this Love, without having to know the future.

● *More freedom.* You will act more spontaneously, take more risks, love more lavishly. By letting go of impediments to love, you will be increasingly free to live out of the principle of love.

And One More Thing . . .

I will bless you . . . so that you will be a blessing. (Gen 12:2)

And where will the art of letting go take us? To a life of joy and blessing—blessing not defined by the material, but by the meaningful. And this kind of blessing moves outward, just as this verse in Genesis reminds us. There is endless flow; there is purpose; there is Life. It spills over into the lives of others and just keeps on blessing, long after it leaves our little orbit.

I believe deeply—dare I say, "I *know*"?—that there is a Love out there greater than any leap our minds can make, a Mystery that is beyond us, yet a part of us, that is willing to guide us through all the minefields of letting go. We can discover the myriad forms of resistance within our souls and through the art of letting go, be free to participate in the love of God for the world.

Because the very Love that invites us to release them is the Love that bears them away.

Part V
Group Guidelines

Though the material in this book will lend itself to individual pursuit, seekers often find both enjoyment and inspiration for their journeys in mutual group support. Whether it's a covenant group of five, a church school class of twenty, a one-day seminar, or a weekend retreat, the fellowship and shared interest can enhance the exploration of the letting-go process.

Following are some scheduling suggestions which may be helpful in devising a format tailored to the needs of your particular group. I am also including a number of prayers, litanies, and illustrations suitable for unison reading and handouts. The reflection questions at the end of each chapter may be used for group discussion if the participants have already established a comfort level of confidentiality and trust. Otherwise, it may be more comfortable for people to divide into groups of two or three for sharing at the end of each session so that conversation may flow more freely.

Long-Term Study—3 to 4 months

Have participants read one chapter per week, coming together weekly with a facilitator to discuss the material. Ideally, the bulk of the sharing would be around the issues raised in each person's journey of letting go.

Opening: Read together the Prayer from Kenya or Prayer for Guidance.

Scripture Emphasis: Select one of the Scriptures mentioned at the beginning of the chapter or choose an appropriate substitute. After the words are read, allow a few moments of silent meditation so that participants can pray about the impact of the words on their individual lives.

Presentation of Main Points in the Chapter: This can come spontaneously from the group as shared leadership or presented by a facilitator.

Discussion: Divide into small share groups or discuss as a whole group if the atmosphere is one of safety and openness. Feel free to add your own reflection questions to the suggestions in the book.

Wrap-Up: Ask each person to center on one particular aspect of the week's lesson that is pertinent to their day-to-day lives. What might they be willing to do during the coming week to expand their spiritual growing edge—that is, the next step to which God is inviting them? Urge them to be very specific. The group may want to enter into a covenant relationship to encourage follow-through.

Closing: Choose an appropriate prayer from those included at the end of this chapter, recite the Lord's Prayer together, or ask for spontaneous prayers from one or more members of the class.

One-Day Seminar Study

8:30–9:00 AM	Refreshments, conversation, introductions
9:00–10:00 AM	Session 1—Letting Go—Why? Chapters 1–4
10:00–10:30 AM	Break
10:30 AM–11:30 PM	Session 2—Letting Go—What? Chapters 5–9
12:00–1:00 PM	Lunch Break
1:00–2:00 PM	Session 3—Letting Go—How? Chapters 10–11
2:00–2:30 PM	Break
2:30–3:30 PM	Session 4—Letting Go—How? Chapters 12–14
3:30–4:00 PM	Session 5—Litmus Test Chapter 15
4:00 PM	Conclusion and dismissal

Weekend Retreat

Friday Night

5:00 PM	Check in
6:00 PM	Supper
7:00–7:30 PM	Introductions; overview
7:30–9:00 PM	Session 1—Letting Go—Why? Chapters 1, 2, 3, 4
9:00–9:30 PM	Evening Prayer Service

Saturday

8:00–9:00 AM	Breakfast
9:00–10:00 AM	Session 2—Letting Go—What? Chapters 5, 6, 7
10:00–10:30 AM	Break
10:30–11:30 AM	Session 3—Letting Go—What? Chapters 8, 9
12:00–1:00 PM	Lunch
1:00–3:00 PM	Free time; exercise, games, etc.
3:00–4:00 PM	Session 4—Letting Go—How? Chapters 10, 11
4:00–4:30 PM	Break
4:30–5:30 PM	Session 5—Letting Go—How? Chapters 12, 13, 14
6:00 PM	Supper
Evening	Games, entertainment, fellowship

Sunday

8:00–9:00 AM	Breakfast
9:00–10:00 AM	Session 6—Litmus Test Chapter 15
10:00–10:30 AM	Break; packing up
10:30–11:30 AM	Worship, Eucharist (Suggestion: Include a closing ritual of some sort to give participants an opportunity to commemorate their response to the question: As a result of this weekend study of letting go, what emerges as your greatest letting-go challenge and what do you plan to do about it? Even something as simple as "bringing it to the altar in prayer" would be effective.)
12:00 PM	Lunch and dismissal

The following prayers and handout possibilities may be used as well as various prayers and Scriptures found in the text.

Prayer for Presence

God above us . . .
God beside us . . .
God within us . . .
Come between us—a bridge across which your Truth can move. AMEN.

Prayer for the Spirit of Truth

From the cowardice that dares not face new truth,
From the laziness that is contented with half-truth,
From the arrogance that thinks it knows all truth,
Good Lord, deliver us. . . . AMEN
(Prayer from Kenya, *United Methodist Hymnal*, #597)

Paraphrase of the Lord's Prayer

Eternal Spirit,
Earth-maker, Pain-bearer, Life-giver,
Source of all that is and that shall be,
Father and Mother of us all,
Loving God, in whom is heaven.
The hallowing of your name echo through the universe!
The way of your justice be followed by the peoples of the world!
Your heavenly will be done by all created beings!
Your commonwealth of peace and freedom sustain our hope and home on earth.
With the bread we need for today, feed us.
In the hurts we absorb from one another, forgive us.
In times of temptation and test, strengthen us.

From trials too great to endure, spare us.
From the grip of all that is evil, free us.
For you reign in the glory of the power that is Love, now and forever.
AMEN
(*New Zealand Prayer Book*)

Wellspring Prayer

O Divine Wellspring, source of life and life's end, in whom all the tributaries of
    life converge,
Take us down the well of our own life to the eternal spring within . . .
    from which all people of faith have drawn.
Water now our thirsty souls.
Through story, symbol, and words we speak,
Through the silences we keep,
Through the bread we share,
Through all entrusted to our care.
As we draw deeply from the wellspring of your great kindness,
    may our lives be a wellspring of mercy, justice, and peace.
AMEN (Adapted from John 4:13–15)

Resurrection Prayer

O God of the Risen Christ, help us to know in our hearts that—
— Hope can be resurrected from despair,
— Good can be resurrected from evil,
— Creation can be resurrected from chaos,
— Compassion can be resurrected from apathy,
— Love can be resurrected from hate,
— Life can be resurrected from Death.
As we celebrate the power of the Risen Christ in our lives, may we reach out
    and claim its wonder, sharing it with all we touch. May we know the truth
    that, indeed, each day is Easter.
In the name of the Risen Christ . . . AMEN.

Notes

CHAPTER 2
1. Judith Viorst, *Necessary Losses* (New York: Simon & Schuster, 1986), 21–33.

CHAPTER 3
1. Rainer Maria Rilke, *Letters to a Young Poet* (San Rafael, Calif.: New World Library, 1992), 35.

CHAPTER 4
1. Henri Nouwen, *Life of the Beloved* (New York: Crossroad, 1992), 28, 29.

CHAPTER 5
1. Quoted in Viorst, *Necessary Losses*, 170.

CHAPTER 6
1. Robert A. Johnson, *Owning Your Own Shadow* (New York: HarperCollins, 1991), vii, viii.
2. Karen Armstrong, *The Spiral Staircase* (New York: Alfred A. Knopf, 2004), 292.

CHAPTER 7
1. Eugene Peterson, *The Message* (Colorado Springs, Colo.: NavPress, 1993), 20.
2. Haven Kimmel, *The Solace of Leaving Early* (New York: Anchor Books/ Random House, 2002), 130.
3. Richard Rohr, *Simplicity: The Freedom of Letting Go* (New York: Crossroad, 2003), 81.

4. *The United Methodist Hymnal* (Nashville, Tenn.: United Methodist Publishing House, 1989), 597.

5. Sue Monk Kidd, *When the Heart Waits* (New York: HarperSanFrancisco, 1990), 61–62.

6. Marjorie Thompson, *The Way of Forgiveness* (Nashville, Tenn.: Upper Room Books, 2002), 19.

7. Rachel Naomi Remen, *My Grandfather's Blessings* (New York: Riverhead Books, 2000), 280.

8. Judith Ann Parsons, *The Clear and Simple Way* (Orlando, Fla.: Dandelion Enterprises, 2004), 67.

9. Ram Dass, *Still Here: Embracing Aging, Changing, and Dying* (New York: Riverhead Books, 2000), 14, 15.

10. Erik Kolbell, *What Jesus Meant: The Beatitudes and a Meaningful Life* (Louisville, Ky.: Westminster John Knox Press, 2003), 85.

11. Ibid., 134.

12. Thomas Keating, *Open Mind, Open Heart* (Rockport, Mass.: Element Books, 1986).

13. Steve Garnas-Holmes, *One Light Unfolding* (E-mail Newsletter). (Concord, N.H.: 2003).

CHAPTER 8

1. Dawna Markova, *I Will Not Die An Unlived Life* (Boston, Mass.: Red Wheel/Weiser, 2000), 17.

2. Peterson, *The Message*, 407.

3. Frederick Buechner, *Wishful Thinking* (New York: HarperSanFrancisco, 1973), 2.

4. Julia Cameron, *The Artist's Way* (New York: G. P. Putnam's Sons, 1992), 61.

5. Gerald May, *Addiction and Grace* (New York: HarperSanFranciso, 1988), 32.

6. Sarah Ban Breathnach, *Romancing the Ordinary* (New York: Simple Abundance Press, 2002), 414.

CHAPTER 9

1. Rohr, *Simplicity*, 81, 82.

2. Helen Mallicoat, *Listen for the Lord* (Kansas City: Hallmark, 1977), 2.

3. Brother Charles de Foucauld, "Prayer of Abandonment," translated by Jennie Palma, O.P.

4. Peterson, *The Message*, 29.

5. Gerald May, *Will and Spirit* (New York: HarperSanFrancisco, 1982), 307–8.

6. Armstrong, *The Spiral Staircase*, 142.

7. Kathy Galloway, *Talking to the Bones* (London: SPCK, 1996), 82.

PART THREE

1. Elaine Pagels, *Beyond Belief: Secret Gospel of Thomas* (New York: HarperCollins Publishers, 2003), 227.

CHAPTER 10

1. The Rev. Margaret Jones, sermon preached at Calvary Episcopal Church, Memphis, Tennesee, October 2004.

2. Cynthia Bourgeault, *Centering Prayer and Inner Awakening* (Cambridge, Mass.: Cowley Publications, 2004).

3. Flora Slosson Wuellner, *Heart of Healing, Heart of Light* (Nashville, Tenn.: Upper Room Books, 1992), 66–67; *Best of Flora Slosson Wuellner*, cd with guided meditations and exercises (Nashville, Tenn.: Upper Room Books, 2004).

4. Jan Johnson, "Journaling: Breathing Space in the Spiritual Journey," *Weavings* VIII (March/April 1993): 35.

5. Joyce Rockwood Hudson, *Natural Spirituality: Recovering the Wisdom Tradition in Christianity* (Danielsville, Ga.: JRH Publications, 1998).

6. Jeremy Taylor, *Where People Fly and Rivers Runs Uphill* (New York: Warner Books, Inc., 1992).

CHAPTER 11

1. Wayne Dyer, *The Power of Intention* (Carlsbad, Calif.: Hay House, 2004), 256.

2. Flora Slosson Wuellner, *Forgiveness, the Passionate Journey* (Nashville, Tenn.: Upper Room Books, 2001), 22.

3. Parker Palmer, *Let Your Life Speak* (San Francisco, Calif.: Jossey-Bass Publishers, 2000), 63.

4. Joyce Rupp, *Praying Our Goodbyes* (Notre Dame, Ind.: Ave Maria Press, 1988).

5. Marcus Borg, *The Heart of Christianity* (New York: HarperCollins Publishers, 2003).

6. Archibald MacLeish, *J. B.* (Boston: Houghton Miflin, 1958).

7. Sukie Miller with Doris Ober, *Finding Hope When a Child Dies: What Other Cultures Can Teach Us* (New York: Simon & Schuster, 1999).

CHAPTER 12

1. C. S. Lewis, *The Problem of Pain* (New York: MacMillan Publishing, 1962), 127.

2. Jerome Lawrence and Robert E. Lee, *Aunt Mame* (Toronto: Cop, Clark Publishing, 1957), 137.

3. Bernadette Murphy, *Zen and the Art of Knitting* (Avon, Mass.: Adams Media Corporation, 2002).

4. Susan Jorgensen and Susan Izard, *Knitting Into the Mystery* (Harrisburg, Penn.: Morehouse Publishing, 2003), 24.

5. John Claypool, *Mending the Heart* (Cambridge, Mass.: Cowley Publications, 1999), 35.

6. Garnas-Holmes, *One Light Unfolding.*

7. Armstrong, *The Spiral Staircase*, 54.

8. Cynthia Bourgeault, *The Wisdom Way of Knowing* (San Francisco, Calif.: Jossey-Bass Publishers, 2003), 79.

9. Henri Nouwen, *The Return of the Prodigal Son* (New York: Doubleday-Dell Publishing Group, 1994).

10. Dyer, *The Power of Intention*, 256.

11. Larry Dossey, *Recovering the Soul* (New York: Bantam Books, 1989); *Healing Words* (New York: HarperCollins, 1993); *Reinventing Medicine* (New York: HarperCollins, 2000).

CHAPTER 13

1. Kidd, *When the Heart Waits*, 106–7.

2. Margaret Guenther, *Notes From a Sojourner* (New York: Church Publishing, 2002), 139.

3. Thomas Green, *When the Well Runs Dry* (Notre Dame, Ind.: Ave Maria Press, 1979), 146.

4. William Blake, "Auguries of Innocence," in *Bloomsbury Treasury of Quotations* by John Daintith (London: Bloomsbury Publishing, 1994), 89.

5. Elizabeth Barrett Browning, "Aurora Leigh," in *Familiar Quotations by John Bartlett* (Boston: Little, Brown, and Company, 1968), 619.

CHAPTER 14

1. Kolbell, *What Jesus Meant*, 114.

2. St. Teresa of Avila, *Autobiography*, trans. Kieran Kavanaugh and Ottilio Rodriguez (Washington: ICS Publications, 1976).

3. Green, *When the Well Runs Dry*, 32–55.

4. Kidd, *When the Heart Waits*, 17.

CHAPTER 15

1. Eckhart Tolle, *The Power of Now: A Guide to Spiritual Enlightenment* (Vancouver, B.C.: Namaste Publishing, 1997), 155.

2. Armstrong, *The Spiral Staircase*, 293.